Racial Equality
in America

GOODYEAR SERIES IN AMERICAN POLITICS AND PUBLIC POLICY
Joel B. Grossman, Series Editor

RACIAL EQUALITY IN AMERICA: IN SEARCH OF AN UNFULFILLED GOAL
Charles S. Bullock III and Harrell R. Rodgers, Jr.

Racial Equality in America

In Search of an Unfulfilled Goal

CHARLES S. BULLOCK, III
University of Georgia

HARRELL R. RODGERS, JR.
University of Houston

Goodyear Publishing Company, Inc.
Pacific Palisades, California

Library of Congress Cataloging in Publication Data

Bullock, Charles S   1942–
    Racial equality in America.

    (American politics and public policy series)
    1. Negroes—Civil rights. 2. Negroes—Social
conditions—1964–   3. United States—Race question.
I. Rodgers, Harrell R., joint author. II. Title.
E185.615.B82   323.1′19′6073   74–20092
ISBN 0-87620-776-X
ISBN 0-87620-775-1 pbk.

Copyright © 1975
by Goodyear Publishing Company, Inc.,
Pacific Palisades, California

All rights reserved. No part of this book
may be reproduced in any form or by any means
without permission in writing from the publisher.

Current printing (last number):
10 9 8 7 6 5 4 3 2 1

ISBN: 0-87620-776-X (C)
ISBN: 0-87620-775-1 (P)

Library of Congress Catalog Card Number: 74-20092

Y-776X-0 (C)
Y-7751-4 (P)

Printed in the United States of America

To two who did their best for law, justice, and racial equality:

Father Theodore M. Hesburgh
and
Leon Panetta

Contents

Acknowledgments xi

CHAPTER ONE
Dimensions of American Racism 1

Rewards of Racism 5
Consequences of Discrimination 6
  Costs for Minorities 6
  Costs for Society 8
Efforts to Combat Racism 10

CHAPTER TWO
Status Goals: Tactics and Overt Racism 15

Tactics Used by Minorities 16
  Minorities as Petitioners 16
  Confrontation Politics 18
  Inside the System 25
Steps Against Overt Racism 27
  Passive Federal Role 28
  Evaluation 31
  Active Federal Role 34
  Evaluation 41
Summary 46

CHAPTER THREE
Status Goals: Institutional Racism 53

Types of Institutional Racism and Corrective Action 53
Economic Prerequisites 54
  Housing 54
  Voting 58
  Juries 58
  Freezing 59

Mapping 60
  Voting 61
  Schools 62
  Urban Planning 66
Evaluation 67
  Voting 67
  Schools 69
  Housing 72
  Law Enforcement 76
Summary 77

CHAPTER FOUR
Minority Groups and Welfare Goals 83

Overt Racism 84
  Establishing Standards 85
  Complaint Processing 87
  Litigation 88
  Monitoring Compliance 89
Institutional Racism 89
  Employment Prerequisites 90
  Employment Skills 90
  Employment Opportunities in Black Businesses 92
Evaluation 93
  Equal Employment Opportunities 93
  Manpower Programs 96
  Unemployment Rates 98
  Income 99
Welfare Programs 99
Prospects for the Future 101
Correlates of Progress 104
  Precision of Requirements 105
  Severity of Sanctions 106
  Legislative Involvement 107
  Burden of Proof 108
Summary 108

CHAPTER FIVE
Desegregation: Successes and Failures 115

Racial Contact Between Adults 116
School Integration 118
  The Academic Impact 118
  Recent School Integration Studies 122
  Racial Tolerance 125
  Life Opportunities 126
  The Attack on School Integration: The Armor Study 127
  The Role of Quality Schools: The Jencks Study 131
Summary 134

CHAPTER SIX
Political and Racial Attitudes: Black versus White 141

Black Political Attitudes: Rioters versus Nonrioters 142
  The Riots 142
  The Characteristics of Rioters 144
  Confidence in the Political System 146
  Attitudes Toward Integration 148
Recent Black Political Attitudes 150
The Racial Attitudes of Whites 154
Summary and Implications 161

CHAPTER SEVEN
Racial Equality: Past, Present, and Future 169

Acknowledgments

Our collaborations continue to benefit from the research, counsel, and support of our colleagues and loved ones. This project was commissioned as one of the series on American Politics and Public Policy under the direction of Joel Grossman of the University of Wisconsin at Madison. Joel's contribution to this book consisted of insightful and forthright criticisms that considerably improved our efforts. Peter Eisinger, also of Wisconsin at Madison, read the manuscript and made many helpful suggestions. John Bing and Catherine Rudder of the University of Georgia improved our efforts by commenting on portions of the manuscript.

Our graduate assistants, John Webster and Gordon Folkman, labored long and hard in our behalf and we appreciate it very much. Linn Woodward, Fran Bullock, Diane Dean, and Joan Kelley typed the various drafts of the book with patience and great skill, and in general distinguished themselves as our ideal of the perfect secretary: one who not only does not make errors but in fact corrects those of the authors.

This book is the latest of an ongoing collaborative stream of research that has produced *Law and Social Change* and *Black Political Attitudes*. We alternate the order of the authors' names to indicate that the studies are in every way joint efforts. Thus, we will gladly share equal credit for any merit this book might have. However, if anyone might venture a criticism of the text, we each blame the other. We have found that this policy worked well in the past and we see no reason to abandon it.

Charles Bullock appreciates the summer research support provided by the University of Georgia which facilitated work on the manuscript. Harrell Rodgers would like to thank Professor Norton Long for providing an appointment in the Center for Community and Metropolitan Studies which allowed an uninterrupted semester of work on the book.

Last we would like to thank two beautiful people, Fran and Lynne, for sharing this life with us and making it so much better with their love and understanding.

CHAPTER ONE

Dimensions of American Racism

Racism has been a wound on American society from our earliest days. Some of the most blatant betrayals of fundamental American principles have resulted from white racism. These events include the enslavement of blacks, the attempted genocide of the American Indian,[1] the national failure to honor post-Civil War commitments to blacks, the internment of Japanese Americans in concentration camps during World War II, and the economic and social suppression of Mexican Americans.

Although it is risky to attempt to define precisely—much less assign weights to—the roles played by various factors in shaping the present, racism is unquestionably an antecedent of many of our contemporary problems. Racial segregation in public schools, high unemployment and poverty among some groups, race riots, and indeed the ghetto itself—all these are clearly the progeny of past and present discrimination.

Racism continues for many reasons, one of which is that many whites fail to recognize, or refuse to accept, that the conditions and characteristics they attribute to minorities are not racial characteristics but are instead manifestations of racism. Minorities tend to live in run-down neighborhoods, attend poor schools, hold marginal jobs, and have limited educations because of racial subordination, not race. Even the personal characteristics that many whites attribute to minorities are vacuous stereotypes, the creations of racism. For example,

1

the stereotype of the black as foot shuffling, groveling, and childish has threads running deep into our history. In the past some amount of ambition and aggressiveness in whites has traditionally been regarded positively. But for centuries such behavior was dysfunctional for minorities. In white-dominated contexts, aggressive blacks or Indians risked severe sanctions, while those who displayed little ambition posed no threat to white egos and therefore were less likely to be mistreated. Indeed, by adopting a role of childlike dependence and loyalty, some minority members received paternalistic protection and rewards. The slavery and reservation systems—both undergirded by assumptions of white superiority—created situations in which minorities could not win and even survival often depended on at least outward conformity with white stereotypes.[2] Recent progress has allowed minorities to suspend this drama. But many whites still cling to stereotypes, believing that efforts to assist minorities are either futile or unwarranted.

Contributing to the problem is that until recently both whites and minorities rarely saw minority members in films and television in anything but caricatured roles.[3] As recently as the 1960s television showed blacks almost exclusively as menial workers or as buffoons of the Amos and Andy ilk. Mexican Americans were presented as dim witted, lazy, and larcenous. Indians, with rare exceptions such as Tonto, were portrayed as savages who, without provocation, warred against peace-loving white settlers. Such media portrayals coincided with the treatment of minorities in popular journals, the news media, and educational texts.[4] History text books ignored the contributions of minorities and used them as foils for white heroes. Custom, geographic exclusion, education, and the media perpetuated the projection of stereotyped characteristics and relationships as portrayals of reality.

Ingrained as these stereotypes are, society has recently started to recognize and attack some kinds of racism. As a result, certain types of overt racism which existed widely less than a decade ago have become less frequent. Although there are still flaws in enforcement (which we will describe in later chapters), minorities are generally no longer subjected to the indignities of being denied public accommodations or the right to vote. School segregation as the product of overt discrimination has been eliminated in much of the South and is now under attack in the North. In addition, racial barriers have begun to fall in employment and housing. At the very least, then, rejection solely on the basis of race is now less common in many areas where once it was standard procedure.

Because federal statutes and court decisions have expanded opportunities for minorities and eliminated some of the most visible examples of "white only" racism, many white Americans have concluded that discrimination is no longer a serious problem. Minorities know better. They continue to be disadvantaged because institutional racism is subtly built into our culture in barely visible but powerful forms. Thus, if racism is to be expunged, whites must become aware of its subtle variants.

Institutional racism is considerably less obvious than overt racism because ostensibly race does not determine the kind of treatment accorded. Downs defines institutional subordination as "placing or keeping persons in a position or status of inferiority by means of attitudes, actions, or institutional structures which do not use color itself as the subordinating mechanism, but instead use other mechanisms indirectly related to color."[5] Included here are practices that appear to be free of racial bias but that nonetheless disadvantage minorities. Standardized tests, which tap aspects of white, middle-class culture, disadvantage poor and minority students. Many firms require that job applicants have high school diplomas and that they pass written exams rather than tests of skill. Many require applicants to be union members in occupations for which apprenticeship programs accept very few minority applicants. All these are examples of institutional subordination. In addition many firms refuse to consider an applicant who has an arrest record. This practice handicaps minorities, because they are likely to be arrested for behavior that the police would ignore in whites. Such widely applauded reforms as civil service employment and the rewarding of public contracts through competitive bidding are also tainted by institutional racism. Where minorities of earlier generations could translate political clout into jobs and government contracts, today's minorities remain hamstrung by culturally biased employment tests and bonding requirements.

Because the requirements mentioned above—good scores on standardized tests, union membership, etcetera—do not mention race and are not applied exclusively against minorities, their racial consequences have gone largely unnoted. Indeed, most whites probably accept such prerequisites as scrupulously fair, believing that they assure that merit and not favoritism is the basis for decisions. But because racism applies white standards throughout society and simultaneously restricts the ability of minority members to begin on an equal footing with whites, the impact of these nominally color-blind requirements disadvantages minorities. The Kerner Commission noted the difficulty whites have in accepting these facts. "What white Americans have never fully understood—but what the Negro can never forget—is that white society is deeply implicated in the ghetto. White institutions created it, white institutions maintain it, and white society condones it."[6]

Because whites are unaware of institutional racism, it will not be easily curtailed. As long as white Americans think of racism only as Klan lynchings, assaults on civil rights protesters by Bull Connor's Birmingham policemen, or "white only" policies in public accommodations, jobs, housing, education, etcetera, little corrective action will be taken to deal with institutional racism.

The difficulties that may impede advances against institutional racism can be glimpsed in data on white attitudes toward integration. As a later chapter details, in recent years whites have generally expressed rather high support for most forms of integration—but little support for efforts to overcome discrimination. For example, in the early 1970s, when polls were revealing that from 60 to 80 percent of the white population favored various types of integration, the Gallop Poll asked whites if racial integration should be speeded up. Sixty-two percent said "no."[7] Another poll revealed that 56 percent of the population believe that black disadvantages in jobs, education, and housing are caused mainly by blacks themselves, rather than by discrimination. In the same poll, 73 percent of the white respondents said blacks are treated as well as whites in our society.[8] None of these findings indicate much white understanding of institutional racism or support for efforts to overcome it.

REWARDS OF RACISM

The absence of greater progress in civil rights is attributable to several factors other than the invisibility of institutional racism, stereotyping, and the failure of many civil rights programs. The most important factor is that discrimination pays handsome rewards, both material and psychological, to some individuals.[9] Some employers, particularly those who hire low-skill workers (for example, agribusinesses), appreciate the cheap labor provided by those who are kept subordinate by racism. The savings accruing from exploitation of racial minorities are passed on to consumers, who obtain less expensive goods and cheaper services (e.g., garbage collection and maid service).

Employment discrimination provides benefits at a second level. When minorities are restricted to menial jobs, competition for better paying positions is limited. When minorities are excluded from necessary training or from opportunities for attractive jobs, the job security and wages enjoyed by whites who currently fill these positions are enhanced. In the past when unions were weaker, factory owners could depress the wages paid to whites by hiring southern farm blacks and bringing them North.[10] More recently similar recruitment practices have been used to deflate wages of textile workers. Therefore some labor unions seek to exclude minorities and thereby contribute to the latter's economic plight.

Politicians also benefit from racism. When minorities are denied the vote, or—as is more common today—when the influence of minority votes is diluted, some white officials are elected to offices that should be filled by blacks.[11] Such situations often result in public decisions that are detrimental to minorities. For example, public jobs may be given to whites instead of minorities, and low levels of services may be provided to non-whites. Similarly, white officeholders are more likely to keep taxes low by assessing the cost of public services (sewers, street paving, and lighting) against users instead of financing them with public funds.

Racism is an absolute necessity for some members of the real estate profession. Blockbusters make fortunes by playing on the racial fears of white homeowners in transitional neighborhoods. Frightened whites sell low and eager blacks pay good prices for the newly accessible homes. If mortgage money is not available from conventional sources—and often it is not in minority and transitional areas—the blockbuster may charge the buyer excessive interest rates.

A broad spectrum of white society tolerates racism and even basks in it because it offers psychological benefits. By keeping minority groups subservient, whites—regardless of their status—are reassured that there is someone beneath them on the social ladder. Racism also insures that there will be a group that can be used as scapegoats to absorb the hostilities, fears, and tensions found in society. Moreover, the limitations imposed by a racist society help allay fears that many whites have of blacks. Fear of retribution by exploited minorities (a fear that has its roots in uprisings of slaves and Indians) evokes support for policies that perpetuate racial subjugation.[12]

CONSEQUENCES OF DISCRIMINATION

Costs for Minorities

Whether overt and personal or subtle and institutional, racism has serious consequences both for the immediate victims and for society. By almost any gauge, minority groups are disadvantaged in terms of income, education, employment, and housing. In 1973, median black family income was only 58 percent of the figure for whites.[13] Comparable ratios, calculated from the latest available data for other minorities, show that families of Mexican origin have incomes equal to 67 percent of the white figure; families of Puerto Rican origin have median incomes equal to 54 percent of the white figure; Indian median family income was 59 percent that of whites (1969).[14]

Using statistical techniques, estimates can be made of how much less minorities earn than comparable whites because of racial discrimination. Duncan reports that black families are penalized $1,430 annually because of their race. A study of Austin, Texas households finds that because of discrimination, Chicanos earn on the average $320 less annually than do comparable white families.[15] These figures are obtained when minorities and whites are compared after controlling for differences in family backgrounds and educational levels.

Much of the remaining discrepancy between white and minority incomes is attributable to past discriminatory practices. Some portion of the responsibility can be attributed to the unequal educational programs provided minorities in segregated schools, in urban ghetto schools, and in reservation schools. In 1971, when almost 80 percent of those 25 to 29 years old had completed high school, the comparable figure for blacks was 60 percent; for Chicanos, 43 percent; and for Puerto Ricans, 31 percent.[16] Poor educations have left many minority members unprepared for better paying jobs. However, until recently even minority workers who had the necessary educations found the paths to better jobs blocked by overt racism. This helps explain why nonwhites are twice as likely to be service workers but only 65 percent as likely as whites to hold white-collar jobs.[17]

The racism that has frequently denied minorities decent living conditions is also an antecedent of the poorer health records of minority members. Nonwhite infants are 50 percent more likely to die during the first month than are white infants and more than twice as likely to die during the first eleven months.[18] Another consequence of minority health is that impoverished mothers, because of protein deficiencies in their diets, are more likely to give birth to retarded babies.[19]

Discrimination has a psychological impact. When samples of blacks and whites are compared, the former are found to have a higher sense of powerlessness and less self-confidence. Clearly these black attitudes are the result of unrewarded striving and repeated rebuffs.[20] The constraints of racism are also at least partially responsible for the recent findings that 56 percent of a black sample, in contrast with 17 percent of the whites, doubted they had as good a chance for success as others in society.[21]

Although the causal relationship is often blurred, racism apparently affects the political attitudes of minorities by producing low feelings of political efficacy and lower political trust in black than in white children.[22] Among adults, political trust has declined for both races, but at a steeper rate for blacks.[23] A 1973 national survey found that 68 percent of the blacks felt alienated and powerless, as compared with 55 percent of the total population sample.[24] In 1973 blacks were less likely than whites to have a great deal of trust in all branches or levels of government, except for the Supreme Court (blacks 43 percent, whites 31 percent). Aside from the Supreme Court, fewer than 30 percent of the national sample of blacks had great trust in any branch of government. Only 11 percent of the black population had great trust in the presidency, and 49 percent had hardly any.[25]

Costs for Society

Black estrangement from the political system is, of course, a matter of consequence for the whole nation. Low levels of trust in government leaders and institutions limit the options and time frame available to policymakers seeking to alleviate problems. Moreover, people already alienated are less likely to accept at face value even well-intentioned government efforts, and this makes the building of political trust even more difficult. The distrustful are also more willing to countenance violent political acts,[26] which could conceivably plunge the nation into another series of urban riots.

In addition to potential political costs, racism creates economic costs that must be borne by all of society. Inferior minority schools and unequal job opportunities have produced many minority citizens who cannot fully participate in the economy and thus have reduced the total productive capabilities of the nation. Also, workers who because of discrimination are denied jobs in keeping with their skills earn less than they otherwise would. Downs estimates that, "in 1965, if Negro families had received the same average as whites, incomes received by all U. S. families would have been $15.7 billion higher."[27] Had blacks earned and spent this additional money, it would have generated demands for goods and service and created thousands of additional jobs.

The inability to obtain decent paying jobs and other consequences of racism are responsible for the disproportionately high numbers of welfare recipients among minorities. White racism must assume considerable responsibility for the conditions leading to the higher rates of family breakdowns and premarital pregnancy found among minorities. These social problems produce costs that are met (at best minimally) by society. In New York City alone, the costs for public welfare—which goes disproportionately to nonwhites—is close to $1 billion annually.[28]

Racism is also in the chain of events leading to the inordinate levels of juvenile delinquency, crime, and drug use by minority citizens. Such criminal behavior, while having higher rates of incidence in poor minority neighborhoods, does spill over into middle-class neighborhoods. If one could factor out the proportion of these acts attributable to racism, the cost would doubtlessly be measured in thousands of lives and millions of dollars annually.

Another cost, and one that falls primarily on poor whites, stems from the ability of the white elite to play on the fears of poor whites and exploit them. This ploy has been used to prevent poor whites and blacks from uniting on issues of common concern. Mutual economic interests of black and white sharecroppers and textile mill workers have been subverted by elites who have told poor whites that "you're better than them, you been born with white skin."[29]

EFFORTS TO COMBAT RACISM

Much of the remainder of this book concentrates on efforts to eliminate racist practices and evaluates our nation's progress to date. Chapters 2, 3, and 4 deal with the two basic types of minority policy objectives—status equality and economic equality. These chapters are organized to show the dynamics of the civil rights movement. Chapter 2 begins with a discussion of the escalation of minority group tactics. The remainder of the chapter analyzes the rising demands for the elimination of the overt racism that has long thwarted realization of status objectives. The federal response to these demands is dealt with in terms of changing from tolerance of discrimination, to proscribing overt racism, to assisting minorities in challenging blatant discrimination.

The subject of Chapter 3 is also status goals. This chapter, however, deals with steps taken against institutional racism. Also included is an evaluation of progress toward status equality to date and a brief commentary on demands yet unmet in this area.

Chapter 4 focuses on an area attracting rising minority interest—demands for equal economic opportunities. It describes and evaluates fair employment policies, which have been directed chiefly at overt racism. Also discussed are manpower and welfare programs designed to remove some aspects of institutional subordination. The chapter concludes with a discussion of the conditions under which civil rights policies are most likely to achieve change.

After analyzing the success of programs designed to remove racial barriers and—at least in the contexts of education, housing, employment, and public accommodations—to promote interracial contact, Chapter 5 evaluates whether such interaction produces the anticipated benefits. Specifically, we discuss research on the consequences of biracial contact for improved race relations and the impact of desegregated educational systems on minority achievement and life opportunities.

Chapter 6 is concerned with another product of the political response, or in some cases nonresponse, to the civil rights movement. Using a number of reports of survey data, we investigate the attitudes of blacks and whites on several facets of race relations and the relationship between the government and civil rights. The intention here is to examine the changes in black and white political and racial attitudes during the past fifteen years and to assess the consequences of contemporary black and white attitudes. Chapter 7 provides an overview of our findings and offers a prognosis of future race relations in our society.

The account that follows is not a noble tale. It describes a nation divided and struggling (often poorly) to extend basic freedoms and advantages to minority citizens. For every success there are two failures, for every act of courage and integrity there is compromise with justice, incompetence, and lawlessness. In the final analysis, the investigation reveals that the goal of racial equality remains unfulfilled. The struggle to breathe life into the democratic principles that we sermonize and cherish in the abstract, but fail to live by, continues. Thus, the major concern of this book is an evaluation of the magnitude and consequences of the gap remaining between ideas and reality in racial equality as our nation enters its third century.

NOTES

1. See Vine Deloria, Jr., *Custer Died For Your Sins* (New York: Avon Books, 1969), p. 60.
2. Perhaps the most insightful and poignant description of this adaptation is Richard Wright, *Black Boy* (New York: Signet Books, 1951).

3. Because most of the stigma attached to other ethnic groups has dissipated, we ignore them in this book. Our focus will be on blacks, Indians, and Spanish-surnamed Americans. The phrase minority group in this book refers to these three groups, unless otherwise specified. Although the three groups have experienced most if not all of the same types of discrimination, our presentation will often focus on blacks. We do this, not because of callous indifference for the injustices visited on others, but rather because of the reality of the research situation. Social scientists have published much less about the incidence and consequences of racism for Indians and Spanish-surnamed Americans. Therefore most of the examples and specific data we include will be for blacks. Although the other two groups have had similar experiences, we do not constantly remind the reader of the existence of similarities. Rather, it should be kept in mind that although our account may deal specifically with blacks, it can frequently be generalized to include the Spanish-surnamed and Indians.

4. See Charles E. Silberman, *Crisis in Black and White* (New York: Vintage Books, 1964), p. 72; and Mark N. Krug, *History And the Social Sciences* (Waltham, Mass.: Blaisdell Publishing Co., 1967).

5. Anthony Downs, *Urban Problems and Prospects* (Chicago: Markham, 1970), p. 79.

6. *Report of the National Advisory Commission on Civil Disorders* (Kerner Commission Report), (New York: Bantam Books, 1968), p. 2.

7. *The New York Times,* November 6, 1970, p. 61.

8. Angus Campbell, *White Attitudes Toward Black People* (Ann Arbor, Mich.: Institute for Social Research, 1971), pp. 4–5.

9. This section draws upon Downs, *Urban Problems and Prospects,* pp. 90–96.

10. Elliott Rudwick, *Race Riot at East St. Louis* (Cleveland: Meridian Books, 1966).

11. *The Shameful Blight* (Washington, D.C.: Washington Research Project, 1972), pp. 93–136.

12. Matthew Holden, Jr., *The White Man's Burden* (New York: Chandler, 1973), pp. 28–36.

13. U. S. Bureau of the Census, Current Population Reports, Series P-23, No. 48, *The Social and Economic Status of the Black Population in the United States, 1973* (Washington, D.C.: Government Printing Office, 1974), p. 17.

14. U. S. Bureau of the Census, Current Population Reports, Series P-20, No. 267, *Persons of Spanish Origin in the United States, March 1974* (Washington, D.C.: Government Printing Office, 1974), p. 7; "Indians Are Found Most Impoverished," *Atlanta Journal,* September 21, 1973, p. 11-D.

15. Otis Dudley Duncan, "Inheritance of Poverty or Inheritance of Race," in *On Understanding Poverty,* Daniel P. Moynihan, ed. (New York: Basic Books, 1969), pp. 85–110; J. Allen Williams, Jr., Peter G.

Beeson, and David R. Johnson, "Some Factors Associated With Income Among Mexican Americans," *Social Science Quarterly* 53 (March 1973), 710–715.

16. U. S. Bureau of the Census, Current Population Reports, Series P-20, No. 224, *Selected Characteristics of Persons and Families of Mexican, Puerto Rican, and Other Spanish Origin, March 1972* (Washington, D.C.: Government Printing Office, 1972), p. 5; U. S. Bureau of the Census, Current Population Reports, Series P-23, No. 42, *The Social and Economic Status of the Black Population in the United States, 1971* (Washington, D.C.: Government Printing Office, 1972), p. 4.

17. Calculations based on Department of Labor, *Manpower Report of the President* (Washington, D.C.: Government Printing Office, 1974), p. 269; *The Social and Economic Status of the Black Population in the United States, 1971;* and U. S. Bureau of the Census, *General Social and Economic Characteristics, 1970: U. S. Summary* (Washington, D.C.: Government Printing Office, 1971).

18. *Social and Economic Status of the Black Population, 1971,* p. 113.

19. Charles Seabrook, "Prenatal Hunger Damages Brain?" *Atlanta Journal,* October 6, 1972, p. 19-A.

20. Kenneth B. Clark, *Dark Ghetto* (New York: Harper and Row, 1965), pp. 63–67; Elliot Liebow, *Tally's Corner* (Boston: Little, Brown, 1972). The effect of low self-confidence on minority school children is examined in a number of works. See James Coleman, et al., *Equality of Educational Opportunity* (Washington, D.C.: Government Printing Office, 1966); Irwin Katz, "Achievement Motivation," *Harvard Educational Review* 38 (Winter 1968), 57–68. A study conducted in Waco, Texas, concludes that among Mexican-American children: "Positive self-concept encourages high achievement test scores; negative self-concept, dropping out." Lawrence G. Felice, "Mexican-American Self-Concept and Educational Achievement: The Effect of Ethnic Socioeconomic Deprivation," *Social Science Quarterly* 53 (March 1973), 725. In Chapter 5 we discuss the effects of racial isolation on achievement.

21. Data collected by Louis Harris and reported in Hazel Erskine, "The Polls: Negro Philosophies of Life," *Public Opinion Quarterly* 33 (Spring 1969), 152.

22. For a review of ten recent studies see Paul Abramson, "Political Efficacy and Political Trust Among Black School Children: Two Explanations," *Journal of Politics* 34 (November 1972), 1243–1275; and Harrell R. Rodgers, Jr., "Toward Explanation of the Political Efficacy and Political Cynicism of Black Adolescents," *American Journal of Political Science* 18 (May 1974), 257–282.

23. For a longitudinal analysis of one city see Joel D. Aberbach and Jack L. Walker, *Race in the City* (Boston: Little, Brown, 1973), p. 184.

24. Louis Harris poll reported in *Confidence and Concern: Citizens View American Government,* U. S. Senate Committee on Government

Operations, pt. 1 (Washington, D.C.: Government Printing Office, 1973), p. 30.

    25. *Ibid.*, pt. 2, pp. 86–91.
    26. See Aberbach and Walker, *Race in the City,* p. 204.
    27. Downs, *Urban Problems and Prospects,* p. 97.
    28. Frank G. Davis, *The Economics of Black Community Development* (Chicago: Markham, 1972), p. 16.
    29. Bob Dylan, "Only a Pawn in Their Game," published by M. Witmark and Sons (ASCAP).

CHAPTER TWO

Status Goals: Tactics and Overt Racism

The quest of minority groups for equality is characterized by escalation: in the tactics used, in the demands made, and in the federal response. During the last two decades minority strategies have changed from petitioning decision-makers, to civil disobedience, to violent confrontations with authorities, to attempts to influence the system from positions of power within it. Minority expectations about the proper function of the federal government in the sphere of civil rights have risen. At first, the demand was that federal law stop tolerating overt racism. A later objective was to get federal officials actively involved in eliminating blatant racism. Even more recently demands have been made for correction of institutional racism. In general, the pattern has been for the federal government to move, if slowly, in the direction urged by civil rights activists.

A shift in the policy emphasis of minority groups has accompanied escalating demands. Civil rights protests during the 1950s and most of the 1960s focused on laws and practices that resulted in blacks being treated as second-class citizens. Demands for public policies that guarantee equal treatment regardless of race have increased. Positive responses to these demands can come in various guises, including statements by governmental units or policy-makers that discrimination will no longer be practiced and removal of restrictions on such activities as jury service and voter registration. Other status goals include legislation banning discriminatory practices of private citizens and prohibiting businessmen and landlords from discriminating.

As progress has been made toward some status objectives, welfare goals have attracted more minority attention. Increased efforts have been directed toward achieving a standard of living for minorities comparable to that enjoyed by most whites. Thus, minorities have demanded better paying jobs and equal pay for equal work.

The distinction between status and welfare goals cannot always be precisely delineated. For example, if school desegregation results in black graduates getting better jobs,[1] then eliminating segregated schooling may accomplish both a status and a welfare advance. Also, minority demands for better paying jobs have status implications in addition to the obvious welfare aspect. If minorities are to attain better paid positions, they will have to be hired for occupations previously restricted to whites. Resultant economic gains will enable minorities to take advantage of status gains, such as open housing and public accommodations laws. The distinction between status and welfare goals, although not dichotomous, is analytically useful for understanding the shift in the primary substantive emphasis of civil rights advocates.

We begin this chapter by describing briefly the types of tactics that minorities have used in seeking equal treatment. Then we look at federal policies directed against the overt racism that has thwarted achievement of status goals. Two types of federal responses are defined, and the impact of each is evaluated.

TACTICS USED BY MINORITIES

Minorities as Petitioners

Minorities first sought to redress racial grievances by attempting to change discriminatory laws. Change was pursued through both the courts and the legislatures. Numerous suits asked for interpretations of the Constitution that would expand minority rights by disallowing discriminatory laws (for example, laws requiring racially segregated schools) or practices (such as restrictive covenants prohibiting black entry into white neighborhoods). Lobbying efforts were carried on in Congress and state legislatures, to encourage repeal of discriminatory laws, enactment of laws prohibiting discrimination, and establishment of programs that would benefit minorities, either exclusively or disproportionately.

In dealing with legislatures and courts, minorities often operated from a position of weakness. Prior to World War II, only a trace of the South's voting-age blacks were registered,[2] and blacks were a significant component of the electorate in only a few northern cities. Even quite recently, blacks were only rarely elected as important policy-makers, such as judges and legislators.[3] Consequently, when filing suits or lobbying for legislation, minorities traditionally were seeking policy concessions from decision-making bodies which—if not all white (as in the South until the mid-1960s)—usually had no more than a token minority component. Because, as argued in Chapter 1, segments of the white majority derive various benefits by discriminating against minorities, the difficulties facing minority petitioners were compounded.

The paucity of both minority decision-makers and inducements for white support were not the only obstacles to minority navigation of the established channels. Minorities at times encountered difficulties in even gaining effective access to decision-makers. Until recently, there were sections of the South where there were no black attorneys and local white lawyers would not handle civil rights cases. In these areas litigation was possible only if a non-local attorney could be prevailed on to serve. Also, there has frequently been a scarcity of lobbyists for civil rights groups. NAACP Washington lobbyist Clarence Mitchell, reputed to be one of the best, often operates virtually alone, while competing interests mobilize corps of well-financed spokesmen. For example, a study of federal education and housing policy found that although blacks were important consumers of these policies, they had little direct input during the formulation process.[4] Wolman and Thomas attribute the minimal input to a lack of expertise, less interest in national than local affairs, and an absence of strategy.

Although going through channels is the accepted method for achieving equitable treatment, blacks have often found this route as difficult as a desert passage and filled with more mirages. Pursuit of rights, be it through judicial, legislative, or administrative processes, may take many years and thousands of dollars.[5] Legislatures often balk at enacting new statutes, administrative agencies have frequently been deaf, dumb, and blind, and relief through the courts often necessitates unraveling a Gordian knot of legal delays. A case study by Parenti illustrates the obstacles that confront minority groups seeking relief by working through the system.[6] He reports on a black organization that sought two relatively minor benefits from the city of Newark, New Jersey—installation of a traffic light and property repairs when building code violations were found. Months of work by the black group proved futile, while whites in another neighborhood, with much less effort, got a traffic light installed in twenty-eight days.

Confrontation Politics

When negotiations with public officials proved unavailing, minorities sometimes took to the streets to mobilize public pressure. By expressing grievances through marches and other physical acts, rather than through legal briefs or proposed legislation, civil rights advocates hoped to attract coverage by the media—particularly television.[7] The protesters hoped that the publicity would prompt influential members of the majority to enlist in their cause. Having been unable to effect change on their own, protesters were trying to activate people to whom decision-makers look for approval and support (the decision-makers' reference groups) to intercede on behalf of minorities.

The first essential ingredient for a successful confrontation is adequate leadership. Some minority group communities lacked indigenous leadership able and willing to challenge the power structure.[8] In the past, white liberals were a frequent source of leadership. Black and white students donned the armor of idealism and led the struggle for equality in many southern communities during the early 1960s, with their efforts culminating in the Mississippi Freedom Summer of 1964. Organizations such as the Voter Education Project, Martin Luther King's Southern Christian Leadership Conference, and the Student Nonviolent Coordinating Committee also sent out activists to spark protests. The eloquence and the deeds of activists affiliated with these groups inspired blacks who had long been docile in the face of white supremacy to challenge racist practices. Outside the South, men like Cesar Chavez and the late Saul Alinsky were particularly successful as leaders of minority protests.

Still, civil rights groups encountered a number of difficulties in mobilizing powerful allies. Protest leaders knew that they had to undertake activities judged newsworthy by the media if they were to reach their target groups. However, tactics necessary to gain coverage could repel either the hoped-for allies or some followers. To retain media attention, leaders constantly devised new tactics. Even when protesters attracted the support of people who could influence decision-makers, frequently little was done to alleviate the conditions that had given rise to the protest. Decision-makers often placated the protesters' allies through largely symbolic gestures or by undertaking minor reforms while ignoring larger problems. Protest leaders who are unable to provide victories for their followers often find their support declining. Thus, decision-makers who delayed by creating committees to study grievances or by passing the buck sometimes defeated protests.

Alinsky understood how essential it is for people who are accustomed to failure to experience success if a viable protest effort is to be created. Silberman, in describing Alinsky's strategy in creating The Woodlawn Organization in the Chicago slums, writes: "[A]gitation itself is not enough; the inhabitants of a slum like Woodlawn must be convinced not only that a solution is possible but also that it is probable; they must see some tangible evidence that banding together will give them the capacity to alter the circumstances of their lives."[9] The nature of the successes needed to fuel protests may vary. Specific examples include forcing a slumlord to make repairs, getting a businessman to employ blacks, or compelling the federal government to intercede on behalf of the minority group.

While some protests sought policy change by mobilizing favorable public opinion, other efforts relied on economic muscle. In some communities blacks boycotted merchants who practiced racist employment policies, formed independent cooperatives, or took their business to neighboring towns. Strikes were sometimes called to obtain adequate wages. The organization of Chicano lettuce pickers by Cesar Chavez and the strike of Memphis garbage collectors—in whose behalf Martin Luther King was laboring when assassinated—are two of the better known labor protests by minorities. Rent strikes have been called to try to force building improvements from landlords.

The peaceful protest strategy proved more appropriate for the South of the 1950s and 1960s than for the North. In the South, local officials rejected black requests and often gave tacit if not overt approval to Klansmen and others who responded violently to protests. Northern policy-makers have less often flatly rejected demands. Instead, they have thwarted them through dilatory tactics, or by providing merely symbolic benefits. Rather than sanctioning confrontations with protesters, northern decision-makers have generally withdrawn, leaving the protesters without the visible opposition needed to generate media coverage.

Violence is almost certain to attract the media. However, it triggered white sympathy for the protesters only when minority members were the victims and not the aggressors. King's philosophy of Christian love may have had little effect on racists, but the pacificism of protesters—even when they were insulted and beaten by hostile whites—evoked sympathy and outrage from opinion leaders outside of the South. The civil rights legislation of 1964 and 1965 followed white attacks on peaceful protesters.

The successes of peaceful protests captured the imagination and fired the hopes of many blacks. These high expectations for accomplishments placed a heavy burden on the leadership. Failure to meet expectations produced impatience and declining faith in the efficacy of peaceful tactics. The leadership that had won the victories in the South—victories that sometimes were and remained largely symbolic—became suspect in the eyes of the impatient.[10]

Young blacks who rejected King's tactics also repudiated the role of whites in civil rights groups. Whites came to be seen as either summer soldiers or as incapable of full commitment to the black struggle because of incompatible personal needs.[11] In critiquing the role of white liberals, Holden notes that they derived their power from functioning as middlemen, interpreting black needs to white policy-makers and advising blacks on strategy. Whites often cautioned that in order to retain white support, blacks had to scale down demands and limit strategies to what sympathetic whites would tolerate. Rejection of this advice ultimately led CORE and SNCC to become virtually all black.

The failure of the old techniques to win full acceptance of blacks by whites led a number of blacks, particularly among the urban young, to reject the desirability of integration. Paige conceptualizes the change as a shift from "moving toward" emulating white society and its values to "moving away" from whites and replacing white values with black ones.[12]

Much of the new challenge to whites was in the form of rhetoric. The use of language to intimidate and humble opponents is a popular ghetto pastime, known as "playing the dozens".[13] During the latter half of the 1960s, radicals discovered that not only did black audiences respond favorably to challenges and criticisms of whites, but that such challenges could also attract media coverage.

Black rhetoric that is openly critical of whites and that calls for blacks to act to secure redress of grievances has been unsettling to many whites. Some demands that blacks perceive as well within the range of political debate have been viewed quite differently by whites. The variant meanings assigned to the phrase "black power" help illustrate differences in black and white perceptions. Stokely Carmichael, who coined the term, explained it as follows: "The concept of Black Power rests on a fundamental premise: *Before a group can enter the open society, it must first close ranks.*"[14] This suggests that black power should be threatening only to those who would deny blacks full participation in society. In a 1971 Detroit sample, blacks who were asked the meaning of black power most often responded with statements that were congruent with Carmichael's notion of racial improvement.[15] Most commonly the phrase was interpreted as a call for a more equitable distribution of rights and goods (31 percent) or as a call for black unity (22 percent). In contrast, whites most frequently ascribed a negative connotation—black dominance of whites (30 percent). In all, 71 percent of the whites attached negative meanings to the phrase. Almost half (47 percent) of the whites saw black power as threatening to whites, a view held by only 13 percent of the blacks.

Emphasis on obtaining for blacks what is rightfully theirs is also a theme in demands of some black militants. For example, much of the Black Panther Party platform is not extraordinary. The Panther platform demands that the federal government honor the legislative commitment made by Congress for full employment, decent housing, and equal justice.[16] Nor should there be anything particularly surprising about blacks arming themselves to protect their families and homes from hostile white intrusions. Moreover, in light of the abuses that police have often visited on poor minorities, it becomes comprehensible that groups like the Panthers teach hatred of law enforcement personnel. Perhaps the Panther demand least acceptable to whites is the creation of a separate black nation. This ultimate rejection of whites and an integrated society will not receive serious consideration, although it serves as warning of the extent of alienation felt by some blacks.

"Moving against" whites has, of course, not been limited to rhetoric. The urban riots of the late 1960s were clear displays of hostility toward whites. These outbursts unquestionably attracted attention, but they were an ineffective means of conveying demands to policy-makers. The major weakness of riots as a means of communicating reform demands is the difference in the perspectives of rioters and policy-makers. A critical difference was in perceptions of the causes of the upheavals. The Commission on Civil Disorders concluded that the final triggering events were frequently trivial and therefore must be seen as the capstone of a series of discriminatory acts. Nonetheless, policy-makers often focus on immediate antecedents of the violence, largely ignoring the inequities that caused the tinder dry conditions that could be sparked by a minor incident. Large numbers of congressmen thought outside black agitators (46 percent), irresponsible news coverage (39 percent), and Communist agitators (20 percent) were important in explaining riots. Yet, as we discuss in more detail in a later chapter, ghetto residents ascribed little significance to agitators (8 percent) or other immediate antecedents (11 percent).[17]

Even when policy-makers mentioned environmental conditions as causes of riots, their explanations were at variance with those of ghetto dwellers. Surveys of ghetto residents revealed that long-term problems—such as discrimination, abscence of employment opportunities, police abuse, and inadequate housing—were consistently cited most frequently as riot causes.[18] The congressional sample gave significantly less emphasis to discriminatory treatment and to government shortcomings in housing, employment, and other areas. Instead, they most frequently mentioned joblessness and idleness among young blacks (68 percent), black irresponsibility (47 percent), and outside agitators (46 percent).

Dexter has shown that even when constituents send written messages to their congressmen, the representatives tend to interpret the messages in line with their own preconceptions, regardless of the writers' intents.[19] Since riots are a less direct and specific method of communication, it is not surprising that congressmen did not get the message. The lack of clarity with which riot demands were heard by congressmen is further demonstrated by their perceptions of what constituted appropriate corrective action. Congressmen accepted little federal responsibility for alleviating social conditions. Only 26 percent supported direct federal aid and only 17 percent supported federal block grants to cities. Many more advocated punitive measures, such as harsher penalties for rioters (61 percent), larger, better paid police forces (54 percent), and more anti-riot police training (42 percent). Ghetto residents, in contrast, stressed the need to improve social conditions, to curb police brutality, and to end discrimination.[20]

Congressmen also frequently shifted the responsibility for corrective action to other institutions. Many cited the need for greater state and local efforts (74 percent), a return to traditional church and family values (73 percent), and private sector involvement (66 percent). Similar patterns of denial of responsibility would probably have been uncovered if state or local officials or business leaders had been surveyed. The absence of recognized spokesmen, and the fact that riots by their very nature do not permit addressing complaints to specific elites, help explain the failure of policy-makers to assume responsibility for deficiencies within their purview.

Even less efficacious in changing policies have been acts of random violence, such as sniping and arson, by blacks. Such acts of retribution do not win powerful allies. There has been no evidence that the guerilla warfare that has cropped up in some urban areas has prompted white soul-searching or support for programs aimed at eliminating the conditions that spawn violence. Rather, guerilla violence has most often prompted support for the police and demands for punitive solutions.[21]

Inside the System

The absence of riots in recent summers and the growth in the number of black public officeholders suggest that working within the system has become the most popular civil rights strategy. To gain spokesmen inside the government, minorities have had to attain a threshold of organization and power. Density of minorities in a constituency is often necessary to this goal,[22] but it is by no means sufficient. The absence of black elected officeholders—even in some southern counties in which blacks constitute a majority of the registered electorate—demonstrates the need for more than numbers.[23] Subtle discriminatory techniques and intimidation continue to keep large numbers of blacks from voting.[24]

The prerequisites of minority concentration, accessibility of the ballot, and local organization are, however, being met in new areas, and this has sparked interest in gaining power in the system. In commenting on this change, black congressman Louis Stokes (D-Ohio) says:

> What has happened is that the civil rights thrust of the 1960s has now turned the corner. In the 1970s the civil rights movement has moved over into the political arena and the economic development arena. . . . Militancy has moved out of the streets and into the system. Within the system you can demand change, you can demand involvement, you can demand participation. You cannot do that outside the system and have any effect on the system.[25]

This strategic switch is exemplified by Bobby Seale, co-founder of the Black Panthers, who turned from urging attacks on the system to running for mayor in Oakland, California. While maintaining the same objective—political power—Seale illustrates how Panther strategy has changed from street confrontations: "We had to show the people we could handle their money better than the politicians."[26]

Julian Bond has warned that blacks' options are to work through the system or commit suicide.[27] Elaborating on the need for blacks to become involved in the decision-making apparatus, Bond has urged: "It is at the grassroots level of municipal, county, and state government where so many pertinent decisions governing our everyday lives are made. If the South is to be freed politically it will have to be remade from the school board up."[28]

With minorities increasingly holding public office, the option of working inside the system becomes more viable. Blacks control a handful of southern counties and school boards, more than a score of city councils, and have seats on an ever-growing number of governing bodies nationwide. During 1973, blacks were elected mayors of such major cities as Atlanta, Detroit, Los Angeles, and Raleigh, as well as many smaller ones. From these positions they can at least raise issues that might go unmentioned by whites. In Congress, members of the sixteen-member Black Caucus are assigned policy area responsibilities, and the group tries to insure that black interests are made known in the deliberations of each House committee. In some state legislatures and other bodies, if the two parties, or two factions, are of almost equal size, then blacks can sometimes extract policy concessions by bloc voting.

Where blacks constitute a majority of a governmental body, the potential exists for realizing some of the objectives of black power advocates. Black governments can run the schools, oversee the police, provide public jobs to black workers, and generally make local government more responsive to black needs. Indeed, given the unlikelihood of white-controlled decision-making units voluntarily relinquishing sovereignty over portions of the nation or of black revolutionaries wresting control by force, dreams of black rule of portions of the nation are likely to be achieved only through the ballot box.

STEPS AGAINST OVERT RACISM

Many of the strategies discussed above had to be employed to win the battle against overt racism, because until the 1950s the federal government left racial matters largely to states and localities. In education, public accommodations, housing, and standing before the law, little had been done to protect minorities from discriminatory actions of state and local governments. A number of northern and western states protected minority rights to public accommodations. A smaller number prohibited racial discrimination in some segments of the housing market.[29] Much of the state and local legislation had marginal impact because it lacked administrative enforcement.

Under conditions existing then it was highly unlikely that even meager state and local government protections could be won for blacks in the South. Minority protections could come only when the federal government proscribed local racist behavior. Thus, the federal government had to be enticed to forsake the role of a largely disinterested bystander and lured into the fray as an ally of civil rights advocates.

In responding to minority appeals for equal rights, the federal government has assumed both passive and active stances. The distinction is based on whether the federal government acts or is acted upon. That is, does an agency of the federal government initiate actions against racism, or does it simply respond to complaints filed by minority citizens? The distinction is not based on type of behavior prohibited. To illustrate, both *Brown* v. *Board of Education*[30] and the 1964 Civil Rights Act called for the elimination of segregated schools. *Brown* established a passive role for the federal government. If black plaintiffs documented that they were forced by law to attend all-black schools, federal courts could hold the local schools to be in violation of the United States Constitution.

Titles IV and VI of the 1964 Act, however, chart a course of active involvement for federal authorities. Title IV empowers the Attorney General to file suit on behalf of black parents whose children are denied admission to white schools. Title VI denied schools federal money if they practiced discrimination. Thus, an active federal response authorizes the federal government to go beyond prohibition and to become involved in searching out and challenging discriminatory acts. The remainder of this chapter describes and evaluates the successes achieved, via passive and active federal roles, in challenging overt racism that has blocked status equality. Discussion of federal efforts against institutional racism is reserved for Chapter 3.

Passive Federal Role

Issues as emotion laden as charges of racial discrimination are usually resolved slowly. The federal nature of our political system, with a division of powers between the national unit and the states, is one of many aspects that check rapid change. Decisions which states have traditionally made are only grudgingly brought into conformance with new federal standards in states where a large majority strongly supports the status quo. Traditional relationships and the weight of legal precedent are costs that are considered before federal decision-makers risk disrupting a complacent majority through imposition of new, stringent standards. The preference of many Americans, and not just in the South, for racist laws and practices has been vividly written in blood with sickening frequency.[31] Therefore it has been a notable change whenever the federal government has ceased tolerating racism and declared such acts to be contrary to national policy. Even though the change in position may be largely symbolic and may confer few tangible benefits on minority members, it may be a necessary first step to more productive policies. Although there are occasional examples far back in our history,[32] the discussion here is limited to instances during the past four decades in which federal requirements have supplanted racist laws or practices.

Overt racism has been prohibited in a number of spheres. Supreme Court decisions have declared unconstitutional such limitations on minority suffrage as the white primary (which prevented blacks from participating in the Democratic primary where the critical candidate selection occurred in the one-party South). The Supreme Court also was in the vanguard in shifting federal posture on education. The Court ordered that black plaintiffs who wished to pursue graduate and professional academic programs not available at publicly supported black institutions in their states were to be admitted to white schools.[33] Ultimately, in 1954, *Brown* v. *Board of Education*[34] reversed years of precedent and ordered public schools desegregated. The legality of the racially separate but (ostensibly) equal schools found in twenty-one states and the District of Columbia was rejected: "We conclude that in the field of public education the doctrine of 'separate but equal' has no place. Separate education facilities are inherently unequal."[35]

What seemed to be a call for sweeping change was muted by the Court's unwillingness to require immediate implementation. Instead, new oral arguments were scheduled to determine the speed with which schools were to be desegregated. In the second *Brown*[36] decision, the timetable for desegregation was defined as "with all deliberate speed." As a result of this deadline, which is so elastic as to be virtually useless as a guide, the courts have had to decide the legality of a multitude of ploys used to avoid first token and later full desegregation. In the second *Brown* decision, the judiciary left to itself the task of responding to numerous future questions about the speed, extent, and conditions under which desegregation was required. The more absolute tone of the first *Brown* decision, while not obviating all legal skirmishing, should have eliminated much of it.

The courts have also been the primary agent of a passive federal response to the demand of minorities for the right to trials by fairly drawn juries. Convictions of blacks and Chicanos have been overturned on a showing that minorities have been systematically excluded from jury panels.[37] However, it is constitutional for attorneys to use peremptory challenges to strike blacks from panels in cases involving blacks.[38] Determination of systematic exclusion in a community has occurred case-by-case; each situation has been judged through comparison of the proportion of minorities on the jury and in the population. In 1973 the Supreme Court ruled that it is a reversible error for a trial judge to fail to ask prospective jurors if they are racially prejudiced.[39]

Passivity has also characterized much of the federal effort on behalf of minority demands for equal housing opportunities. In *Shelley* v. *Kraemer* (1948)[40] the enforcement of racially restrictive covenants (terms in the contracts of homeowners that prohibit sale or rental to minority group members) was prohibited. Restrictive covenants effectively prevented minorities from buying or renting dwellings in the covered neighborhoods, so long as one covenanter objected. More recently *Jones* v. *Mayer*[41] has held that all real estate transactions are subject to the Civil Rights Act of 1866, which guarantees that "All citizens of the United States shall have the same right . . . as is enjoyed by white citizens thereof to inherit, purchase, lease, sell, hold, and convey real and personal property." The effect of *Jones* is to make racial discrimination illegal in all sales, rentals, or leases. An intermediate stage between *Shelley* and *Jones* was President Kennedy's Executive Order No. 11063, which banned discrimination in all transactions involving property that is owned, sold, or leased by the federal government or that carries a loan guaranteed by the federal government. None of these policy decisions has been accompanied by federal actions to go beyond minority complaints in checking racism.

Passive federal opposition to public accommodations discrimination also began in the mid-1940s. The Supreme Court, in time, held that racial discrimination in a growing number of contexts contravened the commerce clause or the equal protection clause of the Constitution. State and local laws requiring segregation of interstate passengers on public transportation, or prohibiting service to blacks in facilities open to the public, or denying blacks use of all manner of tax-supported facilities were ruled unconstitutional.[42]

Since 1964 the courts have ruled that under some circumstances overt racism by private entities restricting participation to members is illegal. For example, reincorporation of a previously public facility as a private one in order to exclude blacks has been prohibited, also prohibited is refusal to allow a black who buys or rents a house with a membership share in privately owned recreational facilities to use of those facilities.[43]

While forbidding discrimination, the federal actions discussed here do not provide for active federal participation in attacking discrimination. The standards are not accompanied by creation of a federal agency to monitor compliance or by authorization of federal authorities to challenge people who persisted in discriminating. They do create a remedy for those subjected to discrimination. But unless the victim brings suit, racism can continue unchallenged and unabated.

Evaluation

When the federal response has been passive, the impact on discrimination has often been limited. Impact studies suggest that, in the absence of coercion or the perceived threat of severe sanctions, people may continue to behave as in the past even after a new law makes such behavior illegal.[44] Persistence of banned behavior is particularly likely where there is widespread and deep-seated opposition to the new law. Where the challenge must be mounted by a citizen of a long-intimidated minority, many victims are afraid to assert their rights. In an area characterized by a history of lynchings of "uppity" blacks, bombings of structures used in civil rights protests, and physical and economic harassment of civil rights activists, an individual would have to weigh the consequences seriously before suing the registrar, school board, sheriff, or even a white businessman or landlord. Even after Congress or the courts have declared an aspect of discrimination illegal, minorities in other communities may hesitate to voice grievances. Ten and more years after *Brown,* many school districts operated segregated systems that had never been challenged.

A second factor impedes equal treatment when the burden of bringing suit rests on minorities. Many minority citizens, because of discrimination in the labor market, are too poor to pay legal expenses. A number of cases, including many of the landmark suits discussed earlier, have been financed by private organizations. The coffers of civil rights organizations, however, have always been meager. Consequently, for each suit filed there were many others not brought because of a lack of resources. A third obstacle to suits by minorities has been the absence of minority attorneys in sections of the South where white attorneys refused to handle civil rights cases.

Where there is entrenched opposition to expanded minority rights, even the effects of winning a case may be limited. In some southern jurisdictions, blacks seeking to register to vote or to send their children to white schools won their cases—but were rejected again for reasons different than those litigated. Another problem has been that some court decisions have been interpreted so narrowly by white policy-makers that only the litigants were bound. For example, the plaintiffs in a suit might be registered or allowed to transfer to white schools, but no other blacks in the county or school district would be permitted to take advantage of the decision. Or, a jurisdiction might continue the same discriminatory practices that were ruled unconstitutional in a neighboring county.

Evidence of the retarding effect of a passive federal posture can be found in statistics on school desegregation and black voter registration. During the decade after the first *Brown* decision, passive federal opposition to segregation produced little change in the South. Five years after *Brown,* token desegregation had occurred in only five of eleven southern states. As shown in Table 2-1, even the tenth autumn after *Brown* found two southern states with totally segregated systems. In no southern state were as many as 10 percent of the black students attending classes with whites.

TABLE 2-1

Percentage of Black Pupils in Public Schools with Whites in the South

State	School Year		
	1954–1955	1959–1960	1964–1965
Alabama	0.0	0.0	0.0
Arkansas	0.0	0.1	0.8
Florida	0.0	0.3	2.7
Georgia	0.0	0.0	0.4
Louisiana	0.0	0.0	1.1
Mississippi	0.0	0.0	0.0
North Carolina	0.0	0.0	1.4
South Carolina	0.0	0.0	0.1
Tennessee	0.0	0.1	5.4
Texas	0.0	1.2	7.8
Virginia	0.0	0.1	5.2

Source: *Statistical Summary* (Nashville: Southern Education Reporting Service, 1964).

In voter registration, passive federal opposition to overt racism, such as the white primaries and intimidation, had more effect than *Brown* did in education, although the impact was still small. From 1940 to 1947 (white primaries were finally judged illegal in 1944, regardless of how disguised), black registration in the South doubled (see Table 2-2). During the next decade it doubled again. Despite these increases, only a quarter of the South's voting-age blacks were registered as recently as 1958.

In both education and political participation, prohibitions of previously tolerated discrimination produced some changes. Compared with conditions that had existed for generations, the changes may even appear impressive at times. However, compared with what could be achieved and with what has been achieved in the wake of more aggressive federal efforts, the progress of the passive era seems slight.

TABLE 2-2

Voting-Age Black Southerners Registered to Vote

Year	Number (in millions)	Percent
1940	.25	5
1947	.60	12
1952	1.01	20
1956	1.24	25
1958	1.27	25

Source: Donald R. Matthews and James W. Prothro, *Negroes and the New Southern Politics* (New York: Harcourt Brace Jovanovich, 1966), p. 18.

Active Federal Role

In some aspects of the struggle for status equality federal authorities have become aggressive, searching for instances of unlawful racism and acting against them. Four approaches have been taken: (1) authorizing the United States Attorney General to bring suits on behalf of victims of discrimination; (2) providing for supplanting the traditional discretion of recalcitrant local authorities with federal standards; (3) authorizing agencies or courts to engage in the ongoing monitoring of compliance activities; and (4) legislating establishment and enforcement of minority rights in the private sector.

Filing suits. When the Attorney General prosecutes, minorities are spared substantial expense, and this may mean that more suits will be brought. Because of the demanding recruitment standards of the Department of Justice, suits filed by federal attorneys may provide plaintiffs with more talented representation than they would otherwise have. Moreover, the involvement of sympathetic federal officials may encourage previously intimidated minority members to file complaints or to offer testimony concerning discrimination. Justice Department involvement has been authorized where discrimination prevents political participation (1957, 1960, 1964, and 1965 acts), school desegregation (1964), open housing (1968), access to public accommodations and public facilities (1964), and employment (1964), and when it results in systematic exclusion of minorities from juries (1968).

Even after Congress sanctions Justice Department prosecution, the Attorney General does not have to act on the complaints he receives. Between fiscal year 1959 and 1972, the Civil Rights Division received 37,758 complaints but filed only 2,794 cases.[45] Suit filing varies greatly by subject matter (see Table 2-3). Since the Justice Department was authorized to

TABLE 2-3

Justice Department Suits Filed

	Fiscal Year						1967–1972
	1967	1968	1969	1970	1971	1972	
Education	57	25	36	58	36	16	228
Employment	10	26	20	10	18	34	118
Housing	1	2	12	40	42	16	113
Public accommodations and public facilities	56	26	45	25	37	38	227
Voting	9	4	3	5	15	17	53
Interference with civil rights	8	11	29	51	50	38	187
Miscellaneous	3	4	1	0	8	3	19
Total	144	98	146	189	206	162	945

Sources: *Annual Reports of the Attorney General of the United States, 1969* (Washington, D.C.: Government Printing Office, 1969), p. 43; *Annual Reports of the Attorney General of the United States, 1972* (Washington, D.C.: Government Printing Office, 1972), p. 86.

bring suits against employers and schools, 118 suits have been filed in the first category and 228 in the second. Even though racial segregation is more extensive in housing than in any other context in which the Attorney General may bring suit, little action has occurred in this sphere. Between fiscal 1967 and 1972, the Housing Division filed only 113 suits.

Justice suits charging interference with civil rights have been useful weapons against those who use violence to intimidate or punish minorities. Between fiscal 1964 and 1970, almost 70 percent of these types of cases involved illegal assaults.[46] A number of the defendants were policemen or jailers. Suits charged police with beating or killing minority prisoners and with the unlawful shootings of Mexican nationals. Criminal interference with civil rights has also been charged against employers of migrant laborers, who were convicted of involuntary servitude. Other suits have been brought against people seeking to prevent busing to achieve desegregation. Defendants have been charged with bombing school buses and with tarring and feathering a school principal.

The 1957 Civil Rights Act, the first to authorize suits by the Attorney General, was so deficient that in the first two years only three suits were filed under it.[47] The 1960 Civil Rights Act corrected some of the difficulties of the earlier statute. Registrars were ordered to maintain voting records for a minimum of twenty-two months and to make those records available to federal investigators. Research using these documents produced forty-four Justice Department suits against southern registrars between 1960 and 1963.[48] If the Justice Department won an injunction against a registrar, the 1960 law authorized a second suit to determine whether a pattern of discrimination existed. If such a pattern is found, blacks qualified to vote in the county can seek a court order directing the registrar to enroll them as voters. The 1960 law also resolved the problem of counties in which the registrar resigned, leaving no one on whom federal prosecutors could serve papers. The state was made answerable under such conditions.

Supplanting local authority. The discretion of local public authorities has been limited by two techniques. One method has been to transfer, or threaten to transfer, some functions from local officials to federal agents. The second has been for federal officers or judges to establish numerical desegregation standards that local officials must meet.

Voting rights was the first sphere in which Congress sanctioned assumption of a traditional local function by federal officers. The 1960 Civil Rights Act authorized federal judges and special referees to register voters if a pattern or practice of discrimination existed. The 1960 authorization was not widely implemented, but it presaged the dispatch of federal voting examiners pursuant to the 1965 Voting Rights Act. Under the 1965 statute, counties in seven southern states—where less than half of the voting-age population was registered or voted in 1964—were subject to federal take-over of registration. Examiners registered 150,000 black voters who had been illegally rejected in fifty-seven counties in the first three years after passage of the Act. Temporary transferal of the registration process to federal appointees was sufficient to prompt some registrars—who had adamantly opposed black voting—to begin signing up blacks.

The 1964 Civil Rights Act involved the federal government on a large scale in local school administration. Public schools and other recipients of federal funds were to lose these moneys if they continued to segregate. To oversee compliance, the Office for Civil Rights (OCR) was created in the Department of Health, Education, and Welfare (HEW). The Office for Civil Rights promulgated guidelines specifying the changes that were necessary if a school district was to continue receiving federal funds. The acceptable minimum rose year by year until, by the fall of 1969, southern school districts were required to eliminate dual school systems.[49] Loss of federal aid was not an idle threat. In all, OCR terminated federal funds in more than 250 noncompliant districts.

Generally, as guidelines became more demanding, OCR

came to play a more active role. The Office for Civil Rights has worked both at eliminating dual school systems and at challenging the discrimination that frequently persists in schools even after the merger of black and white facilities. The agency has helped school systems devise desegregation plans and has noted areas in which desegregation remains incomplete. Its requirements have often been quite specific, setting forth desegregation plans and the numbers of teachers to be transferred in order to meet standards.

Another form of federal involvement in local personnel policies has been for administrators or judges to prescribe the number or proportion of minority workers who must be hired. As a part of some desegregation plans, OCR has negotiated with school boards agreements providing that a specific share of teachers hired in the future will be black. In an attempt to ameliorate police department racism, courts have ordered some cities and states to hire a specified number of minority patrolmen each year until the racial composition of the police force matches that of the city.[50]

Monitoring. To counter the frequent resourcefulness and tenacity of racists, federal authorities have at times provided for continuing oversight of compliance activity. Potentially one of the most effective techniques is to require that data needed to measure desegregation progress be filed with the federal monitoring agency. The Office for Civil Rights collects annual data on pupil and faculty desegregation. The Department of Housing and Urban Development compiles statistics on minority participation in housing programs. Congress has authorized enumerations of black political participation, but these have not been funded. Fortunately private groups, particularly the Voter Education Project, partially fill this void.

Data collection has been augmented by on-site visits. The 1965 Voting Rights Act authorized federal poll watchers to monitor election day activity in counties that had small registrations or turnouts in 1964. Employees from OCR visit school districts to determine adequacy of compliance. In recent years, visits have usually been made in conjunction with district applications for federal funds to facilitate desegregation. In approving Emergency School Aid Act (ESAA) applicants, OCR uses a check sheet that covers several aspects of desegregation.

In school districts that have desegregated pursuant to suits by the Attorney General, the Justice Department has the primary responsibility for compliance. At one time many school districts involved in federal suits were required to undertake less desegregation than were districts subject to OCR.[51] The differences seem to have been moderated. Courts are now keeping suits open, so that new charges of discrimination can be dealt with promptly. School districts may also be ordered to file progress reports with the district court. The decision in *U.S. v. Georgia*,[52] a suit against the Georgia Department of Education and eighty-one school districts, is open-ended in two senses. New charges and new defendants (that is, additional school districts) can be added to the original suit.

There has also been a tightening of judicial standards. Until the late 1960s, many southern districts operated under freedom-of-choice plans. These were acceptable to the courts but generally produced little desegregation because few blacks opted to attend white schools. In *Green v. New Kent County School Board*,[53] freedom of choice was judged insufficient if alternative means would produce greater desegregation. The *Green* decision and OCR's 1968 guidelines established comparable and more demanding standards for both sets of enforcers.

Since the late 1960s there has been evidence that some courts are more aggressive than OCR in pursuing segregation. In *Alexander v. Holmes* (1969), the Supreme Court rejected HEW Secretary Finch's plea that thirty-three Mississippi districts be given additional time to formulate terminal desegregation plans.[54] Substituting immediacy for all deliberate speed, the Court ordered desegregation in midyear. In *Adams v. Richardson*,[55] the courts demanded higher standards of OCR. The *Adams* decision found that OCR's monitoring procedures were inadequate because they failed to deny federal funds to 74 noncompliant districts, to 42 districts that tolerated illegal racial variations among schools, and to 640 districts that had agreed to court desegregation orders but had not been monitored. The judge hearing the case ruled that OCR reliance on voluntary compliance, rather than taking a more active role, was inadequate. The judge noted a record replete with instances where OCR's efforts to achieve voluntary compliance had been unsuccessful. Therefore, OCR cannot permit further federal assistance in violation of the 1964 statute and must begin efforts to cut off funds through administrative enforcement or by other legal means.

Private sector. The 1960s witnessed the assumption of a more active federal role in regulating some aspects of private behavior. In each situation discussed here, federal statutes prohibited discriminatory activities of private citizens and authorized intervention by the Justice Department on behalf of aggrieved minorities.

Title II of the 1964 Civil Rights Act greatly limited the discretion of those offering public accommodations. Racial discrimination is prohibited in all businesses (those offering lodging, food, entertainment, etcetera) that serve people in interstate travel or that receive a substantial proportion of the goods they use via interstate commerce. Prior to this legislation, the private sector was covered only on a showing of state action—that is, the state was responsible for the discrimination.

The private housing market became subject to a federal open housing law in 1968. That legislation regulates 80 percent of the housing market, excluding only certain types of sales by owners and rentals in small, owner-occupied units. Realtors, landlords, bankers and other mortgagees, and builders are required to conduct their businesses free of discrimination. The Open Housing Act also forbids the use of scare tactics, harassment, and other techniques associated with blockbusting. This legislation seeks to enable minorities to live wherever they can afford to rent or buy.

As the act applies to financiers, it seeks to make mortgage money available to minorities on the same conditions as it is offered to whites. This should help minorities who want to buy in white neighborhoods as well as those who want to buy in minority communities. Traditionally conventional loans and federal loan guarantees have been denied purchasers in poor sections. The consequence has been that many minority home buyers in sections that are red-lined by bankers and federal lending agencies have had to borrow money at usurious rates.

The Department of Housing and Urban Development was designated to receive and attempt resolution of charges of housing discrimination. If HUD efforts at "conference, conciliation, and persuasion" fail, the complaint can be referred to the Justice Department for prosecution. Federal action has also been authorized to cover diverse types of economic coercion: loss of jobs, termination of sharecropping agreements, refusals to do business with blacks, cancellations of or refusals to make loans, and inducing others not to do business with black registrants. In 1968 these acts were incorporated into the federal criminal code.

Evaluation

It is sometimes difficult to isolate the effects of the federal shift from a passive to an active role in combating overt racism. Except in voting rights and school desegregation, the more vigorous attack on overt racism came at or about the same time that federal law was marshaled against aspects of institutional racism. Morover, a scarcity of data thwarts attempts to judge the impact of different federal actions, except in political and educational rights.

Seven hundred thousand additional blacks were added to the voting rolls of the South between 1960 and 1964. In many counties that had steadfastly refused to permit blacks to register, several things occurred during this period. Federal suits doubtless encouraged blacks to make renewed efforts in many counties not visited by federal attorneys. This was also a period of extensive voter registration efforts by the Voter Education Project and other civil rights groups. Justice Department aggressiveness probably prompted registrars who had not been sued—and who hoped to avoid legal battles—to permit qualified blacks to register. Successes of Justice Department suits and private efforts stimulated other blacks to try to register. Thus, the movement fed on its successes.

These gains notwithstanding, obstacles remain. Although even civil rights organizations agree that "absolute refusals to allow black registration are no longer encountered,"[56] they note some discriminatory acts. Also, intimidation, although less common, still occurs in some areas.

As the federal government became a more active opponent

TABLE 2-4

Percentage of Black Pupils in Public Schools with Whites in Selected Southern States

State	School Year	
	1963–1964	1968–1969
Alabama	0.0[a]	7.4
Georgia	0.1	14.2
Louisiana	0.1	8.8
Mississippi	0.0	7.1
North Carolina	0.5	27.8
South Carolina	0.0[a]	14.9
Virginia	1.6	25.7

[a]Fewer than 0.01 percent of the state's black pupils attended school with whites.

Source: Commission on Civil Rights, *U.S. Federal Enforcement of School Desegregation* (Washington, D.C.: Government Printing Office, 1969), p. 31.

of school racism, greater desegregation resulted. By 1968, 18.4 percent of the South's black students were attending majority white schools. Table 2-4 presents data showing the increase in black pupils attending desegregated schools in seven states between fall 1963 and fall 1968. The gains are startling compared with 1963 and with the earlier figures in Table 2-1.

With the demise of freedom-of-choice plans and the resultant extirpation of dual school systems in almost all rural districts, measures of school desegregation show accelerated improvement. In the fall of 1968, less than one-fifth of the South's black students were in majority white schools, and more than two-thirds attended all-black schools (see Table 2-5). Two years later, 39.1 percent of the black students were in majority

TABLE 2-5

Percentage of Black Pupils by Geographic Area Attending School: Fall, 1968, 1970 and 1972

		Percent Blacks Attending Schools That Are:		
		0–49.9% Minority	50–99% Minority	100% Minority
Continental U.S.	1968	23.4	36.9	39.7
	1970	33.1	52.9	14.0
	1972	36.8	52.3	10.9
South	1968	18.4	13.6	68.0
	1970	39.1	46.8	14.1
	1972	44.4	46.4	9.2
North and West	1968	27.6	60.1	12.3
	1970	27.5	60.6	11.9
	1972	29.1	60.9	10.0
Border and D.C.	1968	28.4	46.4	25.2
	1970	29.8	47.1	23.1
	1972	33.8	43.3	22.9

Source: U.S. Department of Health, Education, and Welfare newsreleases, June 18, 1971 and April 12, 1973.

white schools and only 14.1 percent remained in one-race schools. By 1972, 44.4 percent of the South's blacks were in majority white schools and fewer than 10 percent had no white classmates.

The gains in the South are impressive from several perspectives. More desegregation was achieved between 1968 and 1970 than in the fourteen previous years. This is particularly significant when you realize that strides to eliminate dual schools were greatest in rural areas. Although the urban South is generally less conservative and was the site of the first desegregation in schools, public accommodations, and employment, racially balanced schools were widely achieved in rural areas first. For example, between 1968 and 1970, 85 percent of Georgia's nonmetropolitan school systems—as compared with 33 percent of the metropolitan districts—eliminated their all-black schools.[57]

The greater change in rural districts is largely a product of their smaller enrollments. In small and moderately sized rural districts, desegregation could be achieved by pairing black and white schools. For example, pairing in a district that had four schools—an elementary and a high school for each race—could be carried out in the following manner: what had been the white high school becomes the senior high; the black high school becomes the junior high; the white elementary school houses three elementary grades; and the black elementary school handles the remaining grades. In larger districts, the logistics of desegregation are more complex.

Another way to view the South's progress is to consider the maximum amount of desegregation that could be achieved. In the absence of district consolidation, 35.9 percent of southern black students will be in majority black schools.[58] This is because these students are in districts that are more than 50 percent black. Therefore, southern progress should be compared against a maximum of 64, not 100, percent of blacks in majority white schools. Finally, Table 2-5 shows that by 1972 southern desegregation (44.4 percent) exceeded that of the rest of the nation. That autumn found 29.1 percent of the northern and western students and 33.8 percent of black border students in majority white schools.

Compared to its own past and to the current status of the rest of the nation, the South has come a long way. But problems remain. Many populous districts have not redrafted their desegregation plans to correct for resegregation. For several reasons federal pressure has not been used to secure adjustments that would produce additional desegregation. During the 1970s, the carrot rather than the stick has been used to reduce racial isolation. The Justice Department is reluctant to bring suits, and OCR has largely ceased Title VI actions to cut off federal funds. Field personnel from the Office of Civil Rights have learned through experience that, once a district has been judged to have a unitary school system, it is difficult to reopen the case even if higher standards are propounded by the courts.[59] Administrative judges who arbitrate OCR claims are often unwilling to force school districts to continue to make adjustments to prevent resegregation. Even if their superiors supported attempts to achieve further desegregation, OCR has had little time for conducting Title VI reviews. In recent years the bulk of OCR's attention has been directed toward dispensing federal aid, first under the Emergency School Aid Program and more recently under the Emergency School Assistance Act.

In addition to resegregation, other more blatantly racist behavior has been found in large numbers of districts. A comprehensive study of desegregated schools found that discrimination was widespread in 1970.[60] Because this survey came soon after many schools had eliminated dual systems, it would not be surprising if many overtly racist practices have now been corrected. Nonetheless, there are still districts in which black students continue to receive harsher discipline, to face racial slurs from faculty members, and to be assigned to all-black classes.[61]

The closing of many black schools when dual systems were dismantled resulted in the firing or demotion of many black teachers and administrators. When faculties and facilities were merged, black coaches and principals typically became assistants to whites. In 1970, firings or demotions of black school personnel were observed in more than 150 districts.[62] In Alabama, Georgia, Louisiana, and Mississippi alone, 1,848 black teachers were dismissed between 1968 and 1972, while 1,227 white teachers were hired.[63] Evidently a number of districts were ignoring the *Singleton* requirement that those dismissed or demoted "must be selected on the basis of objective and reasonable nondiscriminatory standards."[64] Moreover, if there have been dismissals or demotions, no staff vacancy may be filled through recruitment of a person of a race, color, or national origin different from that of the individual dismissed or demoted, until each displaced staff member who is qualified has had an opportunity to fill the vacancy or has failed to accept an offer to do so.

SUMMARY

This chapter has had two objectives. First, it has sketched out the types of strategies that minorities have pursued in seeking equal rights. The progression of minority tactics, from petitioning to confrontations and on to working within the system as officeholders, has been described. Second, it has described federal moves against overt racism that denied minorities status equality. Because of the reticence of Congress and the White House, initial opposition to discrimination often came from the the courts. These decisions, while valuable for their impetus, often had limited effect against the obdurance of the discriminators. Court decisions established the existence of rights, but frequently realization of these rights required repeated litigation.

Progress against overt racism has accelerated when the federal role has become more aggressive than responding to private complaints. Once federal authorities begin to file suits, monitor local performance, or participate in designing and applying standards, the attack on discrimination usually mounts. With active involvement, the federal effort can shift from a case-by-case approach to the imposition of uniform standards.

Court decisions can, of course, propound universal standards. But in the absence of bureaucratic assistance in implementation, enforcement is likely to remain sporadic for some time. In the struggle for status equality, bureaucratic involvement did not occur until after Congress acted.

NOTES

1. Blacks who attend desegregated schools are more likely to go to college, have better jobs, and higher incomes. See Robert L. Crain, "School Integration and Occupational Achievement of Negroes," *American Journal of Sociology* 75 (January 1970), 593–606.
2. In 1940 approximately 5 percent of the South's blacks of voting age were registered to vote. Donald R. Matthews and James W. Prothro, *Negroes and the New Southern Politics* (New York: Harcourt Brace Jovanovich, 1966), p. 18.
3. In 1964, there were five black congressmen and ninety-four black state legislators in the entire country. U. S. Bureau of the Census, Current Population Reports, Series P-23, No. 46, *The Social and Economic Status of the Black Population in the United States, 1972* (Washington, D.C.: Government Printing Office, 1973), p. 100.
4. Harold L. Wolman and Norman C. Thomas, "Black Interests, Black Groups, and Black Influence in the Federal Policy Process: The Cases of Housing and Education," *Journal of Politics* 32 (November 1970), 875–897.
5. The reputed cost to the NAACP in the *Brown v. Board of Education* suit was $200,000. Samuel Krislov, *The Supreme Court in the Political Process* (New York: Macmillan, 1965), p. 41.
6. Michael Parenti, "Power and Pluralism: A View from the Bottom," *Journal of Politics* 32 (August 1970), 501–529.
7. Much of this section draws heavily from Michael Lipsky, "Protest as a Political Resource," *American Political Science Review* 62 (December 1968), 1144–1158.
8. For an analysis of the internal and external obstacles that black leadership has had to overcome, see Matthew Holden, Jr., *The Politics of the Black "Nation,"* (New York: Chandler, 1973), pp. 8–34.
9. Charles Silberman, *Crisis in Black and White* (New York: Vintage Books, 1964).
10. See the discussion in Robert L. Allen, *Black Awakening in Capitalist America* (Garden City, N. Y.: Anchor Books, 1970), pp. 21–27.
11. Stokely Carmichael's comments in "Black Power: The Widening Dialogue," *New South* 21 (Summer 1966), 65–66; and Matthew Holden, *The White Man's Burden* (New York: Chandler, 1973), pp. 81–86. A number of ideas in this section are taken from Holden's books, *The White Man's Burden* and *The Politics of the Black "Nation."*

12. Jeffery M. Paige, "Changing Patterns of Anti-White Attitudes Among Blacks," reprinted in *Black Political Attitudes,* eds. Charles S. Bullock, III and Harrell R. Rogers, Jr. (Chicago: Markham, 1972), pp. 97–114.

13. Holden, *Politics of the Black "Nation,"* p. 21.

14. Stokely Carmichael and Charles V. Hamilton, *Black Power* (New York: Vintage Books, 1967), p. 64.

15. Joel D. Aberbach and Jack L. Walker, *Race in the City* (Boston: Little, Brown, 1973), pp. 108–114.

16. The ten Panther demands are reprinted in *The New Politics,* eds. Robert T. Golembiewski, Charles S. Bullock, III, and Harrell R. Rodgers, Jr. (New York: McGraw-Hill, 1970), pp. 263–265.

17. The source of other data in this section, unless stated otherwise, is Harlan Hahn and Joe R. Feagin, "Rank and File Versus Congressional Perceptions of Riots," *Social Science Quarterly* 51 (September 1971), 361–373.

18. *Ibid.;* Angus Campbell and Howard Schuman, "Racial Attitudes in Fifteen American Cities," in *Supplemental Studies for the National Advisory Commission on Civil Disorders* (Washington, D.C.: Government Printing Office, 1968), pp. 47–48; Joe R. Feagin and Paul B. Sheatsley, "Ghetto Resident Appraisals of a Riot," *Public Opinion Quarterly* 32 (Fall 1968), 354.

19. Lewis Anthony Dexter, "The Representative and His District," in *New Perspectives on the House of Representatives,* 2nd ed., ed. Robert L. Peabody and Nelson W. Polsby (Chicago: Rand McNally, 1969), pp. 3–29.

20. Campbell and Schuman, "Racial Attitudes"; Feagin and Sheatsley, "Ghetto Resident Appraisals of a Riot."

21. Martin Oppenheimer, *The Urban Guerilla* (Chicago: Quadrangle Books, 1969), p. 103.

22. Charles S. Bullock, III, "Southern Elected Black Officials" (Paper presented at the 1973 Annual Meeting of the Southern Political Science Association, Atlanta, Ga., November 1–3, 1973).

23. In 1973 there were 17 counties in 5 southern states, for which recent registration data were available by race, that have a majority black electorate but no black officeholders. The states and number of counties are: Florida (1), Mississippi (12), South Carolina (3), and Tennessee (1). There were also 111 municipalities with black majorities but no blacks in elective office. Bullock, "Southern Elected Black Officials," p. 8.

24. Lester M. Salamon and Stephen Van Evera, "Fear, Apathy, and Discrimination: A Test of Three Explanations of Political Participation," *American Political Science Review* 67 (December 1973), 1288–1306.

25. "Black Militancy Turns the Corner?", *Atlanta Journal,* November 23, 1973, p. 16-D.

26. "And a New Bobby," *Newsweek,* April 2, 1973, p. 30. Black poet Le-Roi Jones is another militant who has shifted his attention to win-

ning political control and using it to bring change. Raymond S. Franklin and Solomon Resnik, *The Political Economy of Racism* (New York: Holt, Rinehart, and Winston, 1973), p. 125.

27. "Bond Depicts Blacks' Choice," *Atlanta Journal-Constitution*, April 15, 1973, p. 20–A.

28. Phil Gailey, "Bond's Group Helps Blacks Get Elected," *Charlotte Observer*, July 28, 1973.

29. For a good discussion of state efforts to protect minority rights to public accommodations, jobs, and housing, free of discrimination, see Duane Lockard, *Toward Equal Opportunity* (London: Macmillan, 1968).

30. 347 U.S. 483 (1954).

31. In addition to thousands of lynchings in the South, there are the race riots of the first decades of the century in Springfield, Chicago, East St. Louis, and elsewhere. The entry of black homeowners into white neighborhoods has at times evoked equally violent white reactions in the North and the South. The relentless slaughter of western Indians is chronicled in Dee Brown, *Bury My Heart At Wounded Knee* (New York: Holt, Rinehart, and Winston, 1970).

32. In addition to ruling the grandfather clause unconstitutional, laws excluding blacks from moving into white neighborhoods or serving on juries were invalidated in *Buchanan* v. *Warley*, 245 U.S. 60 (1917) and *Strauder* v. *West Virginia*, 100 U.S. 303 (1880) respectively.

33. *Missouri ex rel Gaines* v. *Canada*, 305 U.S. 337 (1938); *Sweatt* v. *Painter*, 339 U.S. 629 (1950); *McLaurin* v. *Oklahoma*, 339 U.S. 637 (1950).

34. 347 U.S. 483 (1954).

35. *Brown* v. *Board of Education*, 347 U.S. 483 (1954).

36. *Brown* v. *Board of Education*, 349 U.S. 294 (1955).

37. *Norris* v. *Alabama*, 294 U.S. 587 (1935); *Hernandez* v. *Texas*, 347 U.S. 475 (1954).

38. *Swain* v. *Alabama*, 380 U.S. 402 (1965).

39. *Ham* v. *South Carolina*, 93 S. Ct. 898 (1973).

40. 334 U.S. 1, (1948).

41. 392 U.S. 409 (1968).

42. *Morgan* v. *Virginia*, 328 U.S. 375 (1946).

43. *Evans* v. *Newton*, 382 U.S. 296 (1966); *Daniel* v. *Paul*, 395 U.S. 298 (1968); *Sullivan* v. *Little Hunting Park, Inc.*, 396 U.S. 229 (1969).

44. Cf. Harrell R. Rodgers, Jr. and Charles S. Bullock, III, *Law and Social Change* (New York: McGraw-Hill, 1972), pp. 181–209; Kenneth M. Dolbeare and Phillip E. Hammond, *School Prayer Decisions: From Court Policy to Local Practice* (Chicago: University of Chicago Press, 1971); Neal A. Milner, *The Court and Local Law Enforcement: The Impact of Miranda* (Beverly Hills, Calif.: Sage, 1971).

45. Compiled from copies of the *Annual Report of the Attorney General of the United States*, FY 1960 through 1972 (Washington, D.C.: Government Printing Office).

46. *Ibid.*

47. U. S. Commission on Civil Rights, *Voting 1961* (Washington, D.C.: Government Printing Office, 1961), p. 75.

48. U. S. Commission on Civil Rights, *Civil Rights '63* (Washington, D.C.: Government Printing Office), pp. 37–50.

49. See the discussion in Rodgers and Bullock, *Law and Social Change,* pp. 81–88.

50. The Alabama State Highway Patrol was ordered to hire at least 50 percent blacks among new recruits until the force is 25 percent black. *NAACP* v. *Allen,* 340 F. Supp. 703 (M.D. Ala. 1972). Although an increased number of minority patrolmen and officers may reduce racism, it may do nothing to make police more popular in the ghetto. Black and white patrolmen have been found to use excessive force—police brutality—more often against their *own race* rather than the opposite race. See Albert J. Reiss, "How Much 'Police Brutality' Is There," *TRANSaction,* 4 (July/August 1967), pp. 10–19. Nonetheless this move is an attempt to correct the widespread racism found on many police forces. Jerome Skolnick found prejudice so common among policemen that he referred to it as a norm in *Justice Without Trial* (New York: John Wiley, 1966), p. 81.

51. U.S. Commission on Civil Rights, *Federal Enforcement of School Desegregation* (Washington, D.C.: Government Printing Office, 1969), p. 35.

52. Civil No. 12972, N.D. Ga., December 16, 1969.

53. 391 U.S. 430 (1968).

54. 396 U.S. 19 (1969). For an excellent discussion of the events leading up the *Alexander* decision see Leon E. Panetta and Peter Gall, *Bring Us Together* (Philadelphia: Lippincott, 1971), pp. 249–300.

55. Civil No. 3095-70, D.D.C., November 16, 1972.

56. *The Shameful Blight* (Washington: Washington Research Project, 1972), p. 12.

57. Figures computed from data in U. S. Department of Health, Education, and Welfare, Office for Civil Rights, *Directory of Public Elementary and Secondary Schools in Selected Districts, Fall 1968* (Washington, D.C.: Government Printing Office), and the Directory for Fall 1970 (Washington, D.C.: Government Printing Office). If districts that had desegregated by the fall of 1968 are included, 88 percent of the nonmetropolitan and 33 percent of the metropolitan schools had no all-black schools in the fall of 1970.

58. Based on data in U. S. Department of Health, Education, and Welfare, *Directory of Public Elementary and Secondary Schools in Selected Districts, Fall 1970.*

59. Interviews with Office for Civil Rights personnel.

60. *The Status of School Desegregation in the South 1970,* A Report by the American Friends Service Committee, Delta Ministry of the National Council of Churches, Lawyers Committee for Civil Rights Under Law, Lawyers Constitutional Defense Committee, NAACP Legal Defense and Education Fund, Inc., and the Washington Research Project.

61. *Its Not Over in the South,* A Report by the Alabama Council on Human Relations, American Friends Service Committee, Delta Ministry of the National Council of Churches, NAACP Legal Defense and Education Fund, Inc., Southern Regional Council, and the Washington Research Project (May, 1972).

62. *Status of School Desegregation in the South, 1970,* pp. 74–105.

63. Junie Brown, "State School Suit Hits Black Ouster," *Atlanta Journal,* March 18, 1971, p. 15–A.

64. *Singleton* v. *Jackson Municipal Separate School District,* 419 F. 2d 1211 (5th Cir. 1970).

CHAPTER THREE

Status Goals: Institutional Racism

Some rights have remained elusive for minority Americans even after blatantly racist laws have been overturned. The remaining obstacles are often standards, tests, or procedures that do not appear to be racially discriminatory. In order to move beyond the guarantee of equality of opportunity to the realization of equality in fact, steps have been taken by the federal government against some of these forms of institutional racism. This chapter deals with federal efforts to remove institutional racism, evaluates the success of these actions, and finally notes some of the remaining obstacles.

TYPES OF INSTITUTIONAL RACISM AND CORRECTIVE ACTION

Institutional racism became a target of federal actions belatedly, probably because it is much less obvious than overt racism. Indeed, the effects of institutional racism were not fully appreciated until layers of overt racism had been peeled away. Institutional racism is less apparent because, although the standards that produce it separate or distinguish people having a characteristic or quality from those who do not, the set lacking the characteristic is not limited to a racial or ethnic group.

Thus, these standards, while obviously designed to separate or classify, do not exclude *all* minorities, nor do they exclude *only* minorities. Unlike overt racism, where intention to discriminate is an essential ingredient, discriminatory intent need not be present in institutional racism. Of course, there may be a racist objective behind some instances of institutional racism, but intent is shrouded in nonracist trappings.

The institutional racism that has obstructed and in some cases continues to impede realization of status equality is of three types: (1) Prerequisites or preconditions that cannot be justified on grounds of necessity and that disproportionately bar minorities; these prerequisities are frequently economic or have economic antecedents. (2) *Freezing*, which occurs when standards are rigorously imposed on all applicants, regardless of race, but only after most whites have qualified during a period of less stringent requirements. (3) *Mapping*—the drawing of district lines in a way that dilutes minority political strength and produces racial isolation in the public schools.

ECONOMIC PREREQUISITES

The most common form of institutional racism bases distinctions either directly or indirectly on economic considerations. As is documented in the next chapter, minority Americans are found in disproportionate numbers among the nation's poor. Consequently, when access to an opportunity or a good is conditioned on economic assets, minorities are more likely to be excluded.

Housing

The racist consequences of economic prerequisites are clearly revealed in the housing market. Developers, lenders, and realtors have collaborated to produce urban landscapes generally divided along economic lines. Even without overt bigotry at the base of selling and planning decisions, many minority families are excluded from a wide range of neighborhoods. Because of the greater incidence of low and moderate incomes among minorities,[1] they are often denied opportunities for decent housing and opportunities to live in desegregated neighborhoods. One consequence is that three times as many black families as white live in severely crowded conditions.[2] Crowding takes two forms—too many people for too few rooms, and population density in black areas of the city. For example, in Atlanta, blacks constitute a majority of the city population but occupy only 20 percent of the land area.[3]

In the absence of government intervention, the current housing situation will experience, at most, gradual change. Because larger profits can be earned by building expensive homes in homogeneous neighborhoods, few inexpensive units will be constructed and those that are built will be in the poorer sections. These actions all conspire to perpetuate the ghetto. Federal policy has, in halfhearted fashion, sought to improve the housing of the poor. Public housing has been subsidized by the federal government but has never come close to meeting the needs of the poor. Moreover, efforts to improve housing conditions have not dealt with the problem of racial and economic residential segregation. Indeed, public housing projects have often been located to perpetuate segregation.

During the past decade the Department of Housing and Urban Development (HUD) took hesitant steps toward expansion and improvement of the housing alternatives available to the poor and to minorities. If seriously pursued, HUD's programs have the potential both to provide decent housing in better environments and to allow poor minority families who wish to do so to live in desegregated neighborhoods. These programs are of two types. Some are designed to expand the housing supply available to low- and moderate-income families. The others seek to increase the opportunities available to minorities to live wherever they can afford to rent or buy.

Increasing the number of inexpensive dwellings has been the object of several programs offering incentives to the private sector. Legislation enacted in 1968 subsidized the construction and rehabilitation of apartments and homes. These programs enable families earning $3,000 to $6,500 annually to purchase or rent units that they could not otherwise afford. They pay no more than 20 to 25 percent of their income (the higher figure applies to rentals) and the federal government contributes the difference between what the occupant can afford and the fair market value. Mortgage subsidies (Section 235) are paid directly to the lending institution and reduce interest rates to as little as 1 percent. Rent subsidies (Section 236) go to nonprofit organizations to reduce the interest on construction loans.

In 1974, Congress enacted new housing legislation which established some new directions. The primary technique for providing low-income housing will be for the federal government to lease buildings and then rent apartments to low- and moderate-income families for less than market value. Congress refused to scrap Section 235 and 236 housing, as President Nixon requested, but it did substantially reduce the programs' support. A new program included in 1974 housing legislation will involve the federal government in urban homesteading. This program, which has been tried on a limited basis by a few cities, sells abandoned dwellings very cheaply to people who will agree to occupy and rehabilitate them within a specified period.

None of these programs, however, will necessarily do anything to facilitate desegregation. Projects funded under these programs may (like public housing projects) be built in or on the periphery of declining neighborhoods or in the ghetto.

There have been several proposals, however, that do challenge institutional racism in housing by expanding the areas in which minorities can live. Under its open communities concept, HUD sought to acquire suburban tracts on which to build low or moderately priced housing. Residents near these tracts have objected, often strenuously, to the prospect of having socially or racially dissimilar neighbors and to the placing of apartments or cluster housing near single family subdivisions.

Two other programs have attempted to induce suburban areas to accept inexpensive housing by making it a prerequisite for receiving federal funds. Before they were suspended, urban renewal and community development grants were conditioned on the agreement by applicant cities to eliminate discrimination and to increase the supply of low- and moderate-income housing. Acquisition of federal office space is also conditioned on the availability of cheap housing free of racism. Before the General Services Administration obtains new quarters for an agency, HUD must investigate the housing conditions in the vicinity. If housing in the area is judged inadequate, GSA can still secure space, but GSA, HUD, the agency that will occupy the space, and the community involved must devise an affirmative action plan to correct inadequacies.

Operating on an experimental basis is a program that gives a cash allotment for housing directly to poor families. These funds augment the amount the family would normally spend for shelter. Unlike the Section 235 and 236 subsidies, which were usually tied to designated projects, direct cash allotments can be used for housing anywhere in a city. Obviously this would permit minorities who wished to do so to move into white areas that otherwise would be too expensive.

During the second Nixon administration, many of the programs discussed above were suspended. Authorization of new Section 235 and 236 projects was held in abeyance after January 1973. Funding of urban renewal and other urban programs lapsed when Nixon proposed revenue sharing for urban development.

There is little evidence that the preconditions attached to categorical grants concerning inexpensive housing and the elimination of racism had much effect, and one can hold out even less hope for block grants which replaced categoric assistance. The 1974 Better Communities Act does not include the elimination of discriminatory policies as a precondition for funding. And while the Act endorses using community development funds to improve the living conditions of the poor, recipients need not work to disperse inexpensive housing. A prerequisite for funding is that recipient communities show that they comply with civil rights laws. These statutes, however, require only that minority housing options not be restricted. They do not require efforts to diversify communities racially or economically.

Efforts to make it possible for poor minorities to obtain housing beyond the confines of the ghetto have broad ramifications. The availability of inexpensive housing scattered throughout a metropolitan area would do more to achieve interdistrict racial balance in schools than will most plans for school desegregation. The location of industrial and commercial establishments in suburbia means that many job opportunities are located far from central city ghettos. Either much improved public transit or available housing near these jobs will be a necessity if many minorities are to have access to the suburban job market.

Voting

Although much remains to be done about economic prerequisites, the last direct financial obstacle to voting has been eliminated. The poll tax, which by the mid-1960s was collected in only five states, was disposed of by a double-barreled blast. The twenty-fourth Amendment freed federal elections from the poll tax, and a Supreme Court decision held it unconstitutional in any election.[4] Evidence that the tax disproportionately excluded some minorities is offered by Nimmo and McCleskey.[5] They found a marked increase in Mexican-American, but not black, registration in Houston following removal of the tax. Research in rural areas might well have found increased black registration following removal of the poll tax.

Juries

A final federal program aimed at correcting a frequent form of institutional racism that has economic antecedents is the Federal Jury Reform Act of 1968. The objective of this legislation is to increase the participation of the poor and minorities on federal juries. The statute requires that each United States district court devise a plan for randomly selecting jurors. It also formulates conditions for excluding and excusing jurors. The act stops short of requiring that juries actually mirror the racial characteristics of the community from which they are chosen, but it may offset disproportionate selection of the economic elite of an area.

FREEZING

This aspect of institutional racism may be found when overt discrimination that previously occurred is no longer practiced. During the reign of overt racism, most blacks—but few whites—were denied access to some rights. Now, equal enforcement of standards for all applicants forces minorities to meet more demanding conditions than were required of whites during the overtly racist past. Therefore, even though new standards are fair and are applied equally, the effect is to perpetuate the discrimination of the past.

Equity may require that where prerequisites were once applied in discriminatory fashion, they now be dispensed with altogether. For this reason, various prerequisites to voter registration have been prohibited. The 1964 Civil Rights Act was the first step, making completion of the sixth grade in an American school presumptive of literacy. This rebuttable presumption (i.e. applicants who had completed the sixth grade are presumed literate, although registration officials can seek to prove otherwise) was extended to Puerto Ricans and others who were not educated in English. The 1965 Voting Rights act suspended literacy requirements and all other tests and devices in specific portions of the country. Suffrage requirements other than age, residence, and criminal record were prohibited in all or part of seven southern states. Areas covered were those in which less than half the potential electorate was registered or voted in 1964.

The effect of the 1965 law was to allow illiterate blacks to register in counties where illiterate whites had registered in the past. This prevented registrars who had blatantly discriminated —accepting and even completing applications from illiterate whites while rejecting literate blacks—from requiring literacy of *any new* applicants. Failure to allow illiterate blacks to register would have enabled whites to continue to benefit from previous discrimination.

The 1970 Voting Rights Act extended until 1976 the suspension of tests and devices in the areas already covered. This prohibition was made applicable to states and counties throughout the country that had less than 50 percent of the voting-age public registered or voting in the 1968 presidential election. A federal district court recently found minority registration in some New York City boroughs to be so low as to subject them to the triggering formula of the 1970 Act.[6] This marks the initial application of the statute to a northern city. The Act also suspended literacy tests throughout the nation until August 1975. Because the median level of education in 1970 was 9.8 years for blacks and 9.9 years for Spanish-surnamed, as compared with 12.1 years for whites, the suspension of literacy tests may open the voting booth to large numbers of minority members throughout the nation.

The other major application of the antifreezing approach to institutional racism has come in employment. The prohibition of techniques that perpetuate racial differences in occupational distributions is discussed in the next chapter.

MAPPING

The location of district lines has had a discriminatory effect on minorities in voting, education, and housing. Although there are doubtless instances in which districting was conducted with an intent to disadvantage minorities, in other instances where districting was done without racist intent the effect is nevertheless the same. Because of the impossibility of determining the intent of those who draw the lines, all instances of discriminatory districting will be treated as institutional racism in the following discussion.

Voting

As black registration and voting have grown, apportioning plans have increasingly become an obstacle to the realization of maximum black political influence. The effects of even full minority enfranchisement can be reduced by schemes that create districts with small white majorities. Given white prejudices and larger white voter participation, blacks are most likely to be able to elect a candidate when they comprise a majority.[7] The retarding impact that districting can have on black representation is illustrated by the situation in Alabama. In 1973, under a plan that followed county lines in drawing legislative districts and that included multimember districts (i.e. two or more members represent the same constituency), 3 of the 105 legislators were black even though the state is 26.2 percent black. A federal court plan which eliminated multimember districts and follows census enumeration district lines resulted in 13 blacks being elected to the Alabama House of Representatives in 1974.[8]

Federal actions against racially discriminatory districting plans have been most frequent in states covered by the 1965 and 1970 Voting Rights Acts. These states and counties must submit all changes in election procedure to the Justice Department or to a federal district judge in Washington, D.C., for approval. To illustrate, in Georgia the legislature has been forced to forsake traditional multimember districts whenever Justice has seen a possibility that the plan might dilute black votes. Informal evaluations by Justice of proposals for dividing multimember districts into singlemember ones set a very demanding standard. The impression given by Justice is that the legislature has a duty to maximize the number of majority black districts. As one example, the division of a two-man district into single-member ones having 43.6 and 45.6 black minorities was rejected. Justice noted that: "Evaluation of census data and demographic maps indicate that alternative plans can readily be drawn which would result in a 60 percent [black] district."[9]

If the standard of maximizing black voting strength becomes accepted by the courts, it will result in more minority representatives at all levels of government throughout the country. Currently it seems likely that only the handful of states that must submit redistricting plans for federal approval will be held to this standard. If minority maximization for these states is embraced by the courts, it might be extended to other states through private suits.

Schools

Institutional racism has also been discerned in the drawing of school attendance zones. Some southern school districts that are too large to eliminate racially identifiable schools through pairing or consolidation have been required to redraw attendance zones to produce approximately the same racial balance at all schools. In some other districts, zones have been left largely unaltered but students are permitted to transfer from schools in which their race is a majority to ones in which they will be in the minority.

The challenge to zoning that produces racial imbalance has come from judicial and administrative quarters. In 1971, the Supreme Court upheld a district court desegregation plan that found neighborhood schools or racially neutral zoning plans inadequate in *de jure* districts if they permitted the continuance of racially separate schools.[10] *Swann* v. *Charlotte-Mecklenburg Board of Education* legitimized the setting of racial ratios for students and the meeting of these ratios through busing. The Court observed that "Desegregation plans cannot be limited to the walk-in school."[11] Other techniques that could be used in conjunction with busing to promote desegregation are rezoning, school closings, and pairing. The latitude available to the courts in forcing districts to undo past injustices is expansive: "The remedy for such segregation may be administratively awkward, inconvenient, and even bizarre in some situations and may impose burdens on some; but all awkwardness and inconvenience cannot be avoided in the interim period when remedial adjustments are being made to eliminate the dual school system."[12]

The Office for Civil Rights (OCR) has taken a few steps to implement noncontiguous zoning, but the agency's efforts did not have much backing from the Nixon administration. Moreover, OCR has chosen to largely ignore districts desegregated through private suits. Consequently, a number of systems that did not eliminate racially identifiable schools still have them, the *Swann* decision notwithstanding.

Adherence to a distinction between *de jure* and *de facto* (segregation supposedly resulting from housing patterns rather than from law) segregation delayed extensive actions against discrimination in northern schools. Since the mid-1960s, a number of lower federal courts have expanded the *de jure* concept to include actions other than the legal requirement of segregation.[13] A broadened interpretation of *de jure* segregation was embraced by the Supreme Court in 1973 in *Keyes* v. *School District No. 1*,[14] a case involving Denver schools. From *Keyes* comes the principle that districts that have drawn school zone boundaries, located new schools, or expanded schools to cause or promote racial separation are guilty of *de jure* segregation whether located in the North or South. It is immaterial that such actions did not involve all of a district's schools or that they occurred in the past. Tampering with only a segment of the district is sufficient to require district-wide desegregation if substantial segregation resulted from such intervention. Past actions demand rectification if their consequences persist. Therefore, a district that has had a racially neutral student assignment program, even for a number of years, may be guilty of discrimination because of its previous actions. Finally, in a district in which segregation exists, *Keyes* places on the school board the burden of proving that it is not responsible for the racial separation.

The standards set by *Keyes* have the potential of forcing most northern districts with racially identifiable schools to take corrective steps. The 1970s may witness a spread of desegregation in northern cities comparable to what occurred in the South during the late 1960s. An obstacle looming on the horizon, however, is the 1974 educational legislation. In the wake of *Keyes*, northern legislators have taken the lead in devising statutory limitations on the authority of courts to require busing to achieve racial balance. As Senator Gurney (R-Florida) wryly observed, "It is interesting to note that the farther busing spreads, the closer the vote here in Congress on tough antibusing measures."[15]

Although the House-Senate conference committee finally struck House provisions limiting the busing of students beyond the school next closest to their homes and opening all existing busing plans to review, the legislation remains fairly conservative. The conference committee compromise specifies a series of alternatives that must be tried and found inadequate before busing can be used. Although the compromise expresses congressional opposition to busing further than the next closest school, it does permit courts to order more extensive busing if it is necessary to protect students' constitutional rights. The general tenor of the legislation may make federal judges hesitant to order widespread intradistrict busing. Moreover, the list of other techniques to be tried before ordering busing may delay the elimination of dual schools in northern cities. On the positive side, the legislation specifically endorses redrawing zones, pairing, and other techniques designed to achieve racial balance.

The institutional discrimination in education discussed thus far has involved distribution of children within a system. Other challenges to institutional racism in education have called for breaking down the barriers between systems and redistributing students. The trend for blacks to inhabit core cities while whites move to suburbia produces central city school districts having much higher black enrollments than neighboring districts. By 1971, seventeen large city school districts were majority black.[16] Because whites have been moving to the suburbs or placing their children in private schools, the schools in Washington, D.C. were 95 percent black by 1972. Moving in the same direction, Atlanta schools were 77 percent black. Obviously, once a districts' school population becomes overwhelmingly black, no desegregation plan can produce much interracial contact. To achieve a more nearly equal racial distribution throughout an urban area, civil rights groups have filed suits asking that metropolitan areas be treated as single school districts. Some lower courts have ordered metropolitan-wide consolidation, but in a 5-4 decision the Supreme Court ruled against consolidation.[17] Although the Court did not foreclose all prospects of interdistrict busing, it suggested that this remedy could be justified only on a showing that both central city and suburban districts were guilty of policies that were discriminatory. Such a conclusion might be reached if district lines had been altered to promote segregation or if exchange programs had been in operation that concentrated blacks in particular districts.

Minorities have sought more than just the redistribution of students. A second objective has been to free local school revenues from individual school districts and to award them on a per capita or need basis. Because minorities are often poorer than whites, school districts that have concentrations of minority students may have less valuable property on which to assess local school taxes. Consequently, taxpayers in poor areas may bear a heavier tax burden (that is, a higher level of assessment and tax rate) yet produce less revenue than wealthier areas, such as neighborhoods with commercial or industrial developments or expensive homes. Ironically, the poorer areas may have greater needs than the wealthier ones. Poor families tend to have more children per family[18] and poor children may need more remedial programs. Because of the frequent incongruity between needs and resources, minorities have sought a fairer distribution of school revenue.

In *Serrano* v. *Priest*[19] the California Supreme Court interpreted the Equal Protection Clause of the United States Constitution as requiring a more equitable system for financing public education. The Court said, "We have determined that the funding scheme invidiously discriminates against the poor because it makes the quality of a child's education a function of the wealth of his parents and neighbors."

The U.S. Supreme Court reached the opposite conclusion in *San Antonio Independent School District* v. *Rodriguez*.[20] While acknowledging that the Rodriguez children attended financially less endowed schools, the Court found no denial of equal protection. "[W]e cannot say that such disparities are the product of a system that is so irrational as to be invidiously discriminatory. . . . The Texas plan is not the result of hurried, ill-conceived legislation. It certainly is not the product of purposeful discrimination against any group or class." The *Rodriguez* decision halts the trend begun by *Serrano* and followed by several other lower courts. For the time being, there is no federal constitutional requirement that states must undertake to equalize the resources and thereby the educational opportunities offered by school districts.

Federal aid provided under the Elementary and Secondary Education Act helps augment the funds of districts having poor children. However, because the sum of all federal aid amounts to less than 10 percent of the nation's public education expenditures, large differences persist within as well as between states.

Urban Planning

A final example in which a variant of mapping may constitute institutional racism occurs in urban planning. Most urban areas now have some form of zoning that divides the community into commercial, industrial, single-family, and multifamily sectors. Some expensive residential areas have zoning ordinances that require exceptionally large lots for each dwelling. Specification of minimum lot sizes of an acre or more effectively prevents the development of moderately priced housing. Even zoning that limits neighborhoods to single-family development is tainted with institutional racism. In 1974, the Supreme Court approved a zoning ordinance that limited residential use to single-family occupancy.[21] The decision also explicitly suggested that large-lot zoning is constitutional.

Objectives such as low density can also be achieved through private covenants that set minimum sizes for dwellings or lots or specify use of expensive building materials. These requirements, by raising costs, exclude disproportionate numbers of minorities.

EVALUATION

At the threshold of our nation's third century, we see that minority Americans have made substantial progress toward the achievement of status equality. Advances have been greater in voting, education, and public accommodations than in housing and criminal justice. In all five areas, federal law has at the least changed from tolerating overtly racist practices to taking a passive stand in opposition. In voting, education, and housing, federal authorities have set higher standards and have moved against some aspects of institutional racism.

Although much has changed in recent years, there remain obstacles to complete status equality. In this section we assess briefly where the nation stands from the perspective of what has been done as well as in light of the demands for additional change.

Voting

Nationally the rate of black political participation relative to that of whites has risen during the past decade. As shown in Table 3-1, a substantially larger share of the nation's black population report being registered and having voted, and the ratio of black to white participation has increased. Although there is fluctuation in participation rates, the ratio of black to white registration rates has increased monotonically. The table also shows interesting trends when region is controlled. While nonsouthern blacks continue to participate at higher rates than their southern brothers, the same regional difference exists among whites. It is significant that by 1972 southern blacks were registering at higher rates, relative to whites, than were northern blacks, and were voting at the same relative rate. These levels of southern black political participation are remarkable when compared with the .417 black to white registration ratio found as recently as 1956.[22]

Despite the vast expansion in black participation in the

TABLE 3-1

Reported Voter Registration and Participation Rates of the Voting Age Population (percent of population) November 1966, 1968, 1970, and 1972

	\multicolumn{4}{c	}{Were Registered}	\multicolumn{4}{c}{Voted}
	1966	1968	1970	1972	1966	1968	1970	1972
United States								
—Black	60.2	66.2	60.8	65.5	41.8	57.6	43.5	52.1
—White	71.7	75.4	69.1	73.4	57.1	69.1	56.0	64.5
—Ratio black to white	.840	.878	.880	.892	.732	.834	.777	.808
South								
—Black	52.9	61.6	57.5	64.0	32.9	51.6	36.8	47.8
—White	64.3	70.8	65.1	69.8	45.2	61.9	46.4	57.0
—Ratio black to white	.823	.870	.883	.917	.728	.834	.793	.839
North and West								
—Black	68.8	71.8	64.5	67.0	52.1	64.8	51.4	57.6
—White	74.6	77.2	70.8	74.9	61.8	71.8	59.8	67.5
—Ratio black to white	.922	.930	.911	.894	.843	.903	.860	.839

Source: U.S. Bureau of the Census, "Voter Participation in November, 1972," reprinted in *Congressional Record,* 93rd Congress, 1st session, 119 (January 16, 1973), p. E 223; U.S. Bureau of the Census, Current Population Reports, Series P-23, No. 46, *The Social and Economic Status of the Black Population in the United States, 1972* (Washington, D.C.: Government Printing Office, 1973), p. 99.

South, there is evidence that the Justice Department is not sufficiently vigilant against institutional subordination and that it has not eliminated all overt discrimination.[23] Institutional racism seems to be present in the requirement of many Mississippi counties that all voters reregister. In light of the difficulties that many Mississippi blacks encountered when registering initially, the impact of reregistration has been to disproportionately exclude blacks in a number of counties. Other obstacles are the requirement that registration be done only in the courthouse during the course of the forty-hour work week, and the location of polling places in buildings that some blacks may fear to enter. Because of their economic dependence, blacks may fear to vote if the polling place is in the business establishment of a known racist. Economic dependence may also make it difficult for blacks to get off work in order to register or vote.

Difficulties with registration have led John Lewis, head of the Voter Education Project, to argue that because the vote is a right, and not a privilege, no formal registration should be required.[24] Some congressmen endorse registration by mail rather than requiring personal appearances before registrars. Others have criticized the Justice Department for shirking its responsibilities. The Washington Research Project calls for the Justice Department to reactivate federal examiners to register blacks and for federal officials to more aggressively monitor elections.[25]

Schools

It is more difficult to assess the impact of steps to remove institutional racism in education than in voting. Aggressive federal efforts against overt racism desegregated all but the large urban systems in the South. In some larger systems nonracial zones have not been eliminated, although they would seem susceptible to a *Swann* attack if an absence of racial balance exists.

Although urban districts of the South have been slower

than rural districts to fully desegregate, the urban South has made more progress than the urban North. Table 3.2 shows that while 80 percent of the forty largest southern districts reduced the number of racially isolated black pupils between 1970 and 1972, the same is true of only 38 percent of the sixty largest northern urban districts. Even less favorable to the North is the comparison between 1968 and 1972.[26] Data for the South, especially instances in which the decline in racially isolated black students is by more than 60 percentage points, indicate that in most districts it is still feasible to reduce racial isolation.[27]

TABLE 3-2

Changes in Proportion of Black Students in 80 to 100 Percent Black Schools in the 100 Largest School Districts

Between 1970 and 1972 Black Isolation	North		South	
	Number	Percent	Number	Percent
Increased	29	(48.3)	5	(12.5)
Decreased	23	(38.3)	32	(80.0)
No change	8	(13.3)	3	(7.5)

Source: *Fall, 1972 Racial and Ethnic Enrollment in Public Elementary and Secondary Schools* (Washington, D.C.: Office for Civil Rights, n.d.), pp. 12–15.

Like racial isolation in urban schools, another aspect of institutional racism that knows no geographical bounds is the use of achievement tests for placing students in work groups. These tests, notorious for having middle-class bias, judge students less on ability than on past experiences. If the classifications, or tracks, produced through the testing process resulted in compensatory education for pupils who do less well, there might be some merit in the use of the tests. The major federal effort at compensatory education (Title I programs of the 1965 Elementary and Secondary Education Act) has, for a variety of reasons, had mixed success. One evaluation found that "a child who participated in Title I projects had only a 19 percent chance of a significant achievement gain, a 13 percent chance of a significant achievement loss, and a 68 percent chance of no change at all."[28] Worse yet, once a student is characterized as an underachiever, teachers may lower their expectations, perform less conscientiously, or both. Thus, "these children, by and large, do not learn because they are not being taught effectively and they are not being taught because those who are charged with the responsibility of teaching them do not believe that they can learn, do not expect that they will learn, and do not act toward them in ways which help them to learn."[29] Consequently, although tracking has the potential of separating students for special remedial attention, it more often results in shunting poor students into holding pens devoid of education.

The application of ostensibly nonracial standards has also worked to the disadvantage of a number of black educators. Institutional racism is less likely to account for firings of black educators (discussed in the preceding chapter) but may explain the failure of desegregated systems to hire or promote nonwhites. Research in which we are engaged has turned up a number of school administrators who say they would employ black teachers if they could find some who were qualified.[30] Prior to desegregation these systems had no problem hiring black teachers and administrators to teach in all-black schools. Moreover, southern colleges and universities prepare large numbers of black educators. Therefore, it seems that in a number of instances professional standards constitute a form of institutional or even overt racism.

Colleges and universities are also infected by institutional racism. In accepting applicants, universities rely heavily on standardized tests. Some schools attempt to compensate for the middle-class bias in these tests by accepting minority students who score below the minimum for whites.[31] Nonetheless, the overall impact of the reliance on aptitude and achievement tests is to exclude disproportionate numbers of minorities.

Housing

Data available on housing opportunities for blacks indicate that changes comparable to those in education and voting have not occurred. A study of eighteen metropolitan areas concludes that between 1960 and 1970 the housing of blacks and other minorities became more segregated, especially in the South.[32] Residential patterns find blacks confined to central cities while whites flee ever deeper into suburbia.

> In sixty-six Standard Metropolitan Statistical Areas in which more than half of all our citizens live, the white population of the central cities declined between 1960 and 1970 by two million, or 5 percent, while the black population increased by nearly three million or 35 percent. Conversely in the cities' suburbs, the white population increased by twelve and a half million and the black population by less than one million.[33]

If, however, one focuses on cities, rather than on metropolitan areas, there is evidence of a slight lessening in racial residential segregation. Data on 109 cities show that all but 10 were less rigidly segregated in 1970 than in 1960.[34] The degree of segregation can be computed using an index on which 0 occurs when every block in a city has the same racial composition and 100 occurs when no block has both whites and nonwhites. Between 1960 and 1970 the average for the indexes for 109 cities for which data are available declined from 86.1 to 81.6. The change has been slight with, on average, 81.6 percent of a city's black residents having to move before racial balance could be achieved in every block. In no city, North or South, is the segregation index as low as 50.

The residential segregation which the Taeubers found in 1960 remains largely unchanged. Segregation is widespread in

> cities in all regions of the country and for all types of cities—large and small, industrial and commercial, metropolitan and

suburban. It [occurs] whether there are hundreds of thousands of Negro residents, or only a few thousand. Residential segregation prevails regardless of the relative economic status of the white and Negro residents. It occurs regardless of the extent of other forms of segregation or discrimination.[35]

There are several possible explanations for the absence of significant residential desegregation. One could conclude that it is simply a matter of lax enforcement of open housing laws. Such a conclusion may be hasty, because 1970 census data may not reflect the effect of the *Jones* v. *Mayer* decision and the Open Housing Act (both of which occurred in 1968). The 1962 Kennedy executive order and state and local open housing laws (twenty-one states and eighty-eight cities had fair housing statutes before Congress acted)[36] do, however, stand condemned as largely ineffective. The failure of these laws to reduce residential segregation is not surprising, given their frequently narrow scope and the absence of enforcement agencies.[37]

A second possibility is that housing segregation is more a consequence of economics than of discrimination. Even without discrimination, much of suburbia is beyond the economic grasp of most minorities. To illustrate, let us consider Atlanta, where the mean 1969 income for blacks—who comprise 51 percent of the city's population—was $7,296. The annual mean white incomes in suburban DeKalb (84.8 percent white) and Cobb (94.9 percent white) counties were $13,290 and $11,989, respectively. Within the five-county Atlanta metropolitan area, the mean black rent was $65 per month—two-thirds of the mean rent for all area renters. Although mean figures obscure variations, in none of forty-eight urbanized tracts was the mean rent as low as the mean paid by area blacks. In only four tracts was the mean rent less than $80 per month, and in another nine tracts the mean was between $80 and $90.[38] Even recognizing that there are some suburban apartments within the range of some black families, these figures indicate that most suburban housing is too expensive for most blacks. These data, coupled with the growth in metropolitan residential segregation, raise questions about Taeuber's appraisal—based on fifteen cities—that only an eighth to a third of residential segregation resulted from economic hardship. The estimate appears to be low.[39]

A third possibility is that blacks prefer not to live with whites. National surveys, while finding a set of blacks who do opt for all-black neighborhoods, indicate that the number espousing this preference is declining, accounting for only 16 percent in 1969.[40] There is, of course, a difference between an expression of preference for integrated neighborhoods and actually moving into a white neighborhood, even if one can afford to do so. Evaluation of an experimental program that provided direct cash allowances for housing to 205 Kansas City slum families showed that black recipients typically did not consider moving into white neighborhoods.[41] Blacks, not wanting to be rebuffed, may hesitate to test the existence of their rights. Hesitancy may be reinforced by unawareness of the law or lack of confidence in enforcement.

A final factor is the infrequent use of federal funds to desegregate the nation's housing. The Department of Housing and Urban Development, although it has primary responsibility for checking racism in the housing market, has done little to free its own programs of discrimination. In 1971, only a fourth of 289 HUD rental subsidy projects were extensively desegregated, and 31 percent were inhabited by a single race.[42] Segregation has been common in new housing built under the mortgage subsidy program. Some loan guarantee programs also serve few nonwhites, with less than 2 percent of $120 billion in new housing constructed under federal loan guarantees after World War II going to blacks.[43] There was a slight increase in minority beneficiaries of FHA loan programs during the mid-1960s,[44] and blacks were actually overrepresented in HUD-insured multifamily units in 1971.[45] Nonetheless, institutional racism flourishes in some quarters. For example, in 1971 the Federal National Mortgage Association announced it would not buy mortgages in declining neighborhoods.[46] If FNMA considers loans made in poor areas too risky, conventional lenders might reasonably hesitate to make loans in or near the ghetto.

Basically HUD has opted for a voluntary approach to residential desegregation. Goals and timetables for desegregating programs have not been set. Nor has HUD established criteria for tenant selection to protect its programs from discrimination, and it does not monitor progress toward biracial occupancy in housing projects. Use of federal dollars to force communities that participate in HUD programs to expand minority housing has been minimal. Replacing categorical grants with revenue sharing may remove the impetus to expand minority housing options altogether.

A performance orientation may not have been applied to these programs because of confusion at the highest policy-making levels. Uncertainty of purpose is evident in the statements of former HUD Secretary Romney. In February 1970, Romney said of HUD objectives: "The department has established as its goal the creation of open communities which will provide an opportunity for individuals to live within a reasonable distance of their job and daily activities by increasing housing options for low-income and minority families."[47] Although the foregoing strongly suggests that efforts will be made to increase suburban housing options, Romney later deprecated this objective. "HUD programs are of marginal interest to most well-established suburbs, and it is therefore sheer illusion to think that HUD can bring about overnight changes in the entire existing suburban physical and social landscape by turning federal money on and off."[48] The second statement appears to reflect the current HUD orientation. HUD has never cut off funding, *even after finding discrimination.*[49] Nor has there been any movement to make grants contingent on development of metropolitan-wide programs for eliminating dual housing markets and for dispersing inexpensive housing.

HUD has not required affirmative action in its own programs or of the recipients of the grants it disperses. Instead,

HUD only responds to complaints of discrimination. Because of the flaccid enforcement muscles given to HUD by Congress, HUD often must seek voluntary solutions to complaints. HUD is limited to "conference, conciliation, and persuasion" when implementing its decisions. In 1971, HUD successfully resolved just under half (48 percent) of 421 cases.[50] If efforts to achieve voluntary compliance are unavailing, the recourse is to forward the complaint to the Justice Department for prosecution. But reliance on Justice to prosecute produces inadequate results; in 1969 Justice acted on twenty-two HUD referrals, and in 1971 only fifteen suits were brought.[51]

Although neither HUD nor the Justice Department have pursued housing discrimination aggressively, they have demonstrated greater vigor than have the four federal agencies that regulate banks and savings and loan institutions—major sources of mortgage money. These agencies have yet to demonstrate a serious awareness of their responsibilities to promote the open housing objectives of the 1968 Act.[52]

Law Enforcement

Federal efforts against institutional racism in law enforcement have been even fewer than in housing. Blacks remain underrepresented on jury rolls and even more underrepresented on actual juries.[53] Such underrepresentation is frequently far greater than would occur by chance.[54] Because whites are more likely to discount the testimony of blacks than of whites, blacks who are involved in biracial disputes and are tried by white juries are seriously disadvantaged.

A Missouri study found that even after controlling for quality of legal counsel, black felony defendants are more likely to be convicted, and once convicted are more likely to go to prison rather than receive probated sentences.[55] These disadvantages exist even when there is no evidence that prosecutors discriminate against blacks. The finding that blacks, even when adequately represented in court, are still more likely to be convicted, is disappointing because it indicates that some criminal justice reforms of the 1960s (for example, the requirement that defendants be advised of their right to counsel and of their right to have an attorney provided if indigent, and the creation of public defenders in some jurisdictions) are less beneficial to minorities than might have been hoped.

Institutional racism helps explain why blacks receive probation less often, because probation is often contingent on the convicted having a job and a stable family life. Because blacks charged with crimes can afford bail less often than can whites, the former more often await trial in jail, which causes job loss and may contribute to marital disintegration.

Even though blacks are still more likely than whites to be convicted, their position has improved during the past ten to fifteen years. The availability of black attorneys means that many blacks receive more conscientious legal representation than if they had white counsel. "Many observers cite the presence of competent black lawyers in increasing numbers here [Atlanta, Georgia] as one of the reasons blacks have been faring better in the courts in recent years."[56] The growing number of black judges (from 1970 to 1973 the number of black elected judges has increased from 114 to 154)[57] should also save some black defendants from miscarriages of justice.

SUMMARY

During recent years we have witnessed significant progress toward achievement of status equality for minorities. Many objectives of the early civil rights movement have largely been realized. Overt racism is no longer almost universal in the South or elsewhere in the country. For the most part, obstacles that denied minorities the opportunities to interact with whites have been removed. More important, some steps against institutional racism have been taken.

Still, the heritage of discrimination in the South—where early civil rights demands and federal responses occurred—has produced what seems to be a regional unevenness in federal standards. For example, dilution of black votes is a concern in the South but was ignored in the North until 1974. More federal oversight of the South has also produced greater school desegregation there than elsewhere.

What is needed for additional progress is realization that, by and large, the remaining institutional racism is not a regional phenomenon. Standards based on economic, social, and academic achievement, not blatant refusal to interact with minorities, are the current impediments to status equality. Where institutional racism has been attacked—in political participation and school desegregation—minorities come closest to being accorded treatment equal to that given whites. Comparable progress in housing and legal treatment will require forthright stands against standards that institutionally subordinate minorities.

NOTES

1. U. S. Bureau of the Census, Current Population Reports, Series P-23, No. 46, *The Social and Economic Status of the Black Population in the United States, 1972* (Washington, D.C.: Government Printing Office, 1973), p. 19.

2. Seven percent of the whites, but 20 percent of the blacks lived in crowded dwelling units in 1970. U. S. Bureau of the Census, Current Population Reports, Series P-23, No. 42, *The Social and Economic Status of the Black Population in the United States, 1971* (Washington, D.C.: Government Printing Office, 1972), p. 4.

3. Lorraine Bennett, "Housing Needs Attention," *Atlanta Journal*, September 8, 1969, p. 1-A.

4. *Harper v. Board of Elections*, 303 U.S. 663 (1966).

5. Dan Nimmo and Clifton McCleskey, "Impact of the Poll Tax on Voter Participation: The Houston Metropolitan Area in 1966," *Journal of Politics* 31 (August 1969), 682–699. A study of Austin found only sixty-one blacks registered after the voiding of the poll tax in that city. Harry Holloway and David M. Olson, "Electoral Participation by White and Negro in a Southern City," *Midwest Journal of Political Science* 10 (February 1966), 106.

6. Steven R. Weisman, "New York City, Mississippi: Surprising Pair," *The New York Times*, January 13, 1974, p. 4-E.

7. Charles S. Bullock, III, "Southern Elected Black Officials" (Paper presented at the 1973 annual meeting of the Southern Political Science Association, Atlanta, Ga., November 1–3, 1973.)

8. Don F. Wasson, "Legislature Faces Radical Change," *Atlanta Journal-Constitution,* January 13, 1974, p. 2-C; "Legislative Gains Scored by Blacks," *Atlanta Journal,* May 16, 1974, p. 2-P. Similarly redistricting in South Carolina (30.5 percent black) increased black House representation from 3 of 124 members to 13. Jack Bass, "Legislative Session Next in Reapportionment," *Atlanta Journal-Constitution,* September 2, 1973, p. 2-C; Kent Krell, "Once Patsies, Blacks Gain Political Clout," *Atlanta Journal-Constitution,* June 2, 1974, p. 2-C.

9. Letter from Gerald W. Jones, Chief of the Voting and Public Accommodations Section of the Justice Department's Civil Rights Division, to Harold N. Hill, December 18, 1973.

10. *Swann* v. *Charlotte-Mecklenburg Board of Education,* 402 U.S. 1 (1971).

11. *Ibid.,* p. 30.

12. *Ibid.,* p. 28.

13. For a discussion of these cases see Harrell R. Rodgers, Jr., "On Integrating the Public Schools: An Empirical and Legal Assessment," in *Alternatives to Racism and Racial Inequality,* ed. Harrell R. Rodgers (San Francisco: W. H. Freeman, 1975).

14. 413 U.S. 189 (1973).

15. *Congressional Record,* 93rd Congress, 2nd Session, 120 (May 15, 1974), p. S 8143.

16. *Congressional Quarterly Weekly Report,* 32 (May 25, 1974), 1335.

17. *Bradley* v. *Milliken,* .... U.S. .... (1974).

18. U.S. Bureau of the Census, *Current Population Reports,* P-60, No. 86, *Characteristics of the Low-Income Population, 1971* (Washington, D.C.: Government Printing Office, 1972), p. 40.

19. 487 P. 2d 1241 (1971).

20. 411 U.S. 1 (1973).

21. *Belle Terre* v. *Borass,* .... U.S. .... (1974).

22. Margaret Price, *The Negro and the Ballot in the South,* (Atlanta, Ga.: Southern Regional Council, 1959), p. 10.

23. This paragraph draws on *The Shameful Blight* (Washington, D.C.: Washington Research Project, 1972).

24. "Voter Registration in Dixie Criticized," *Atlanta Journal,* October 23, 1972, p. 2-A.

25. *Shameful Blight,* p. vii.

26. Between 1968 and 1972, 92 percent of the South's largest school districts reduced racial isolation while an increase occurred in only one district (3 percent). Data for the North's largest districts show increased racial isolation in 42 percent of the districts and a decline in 44 percent. The more pronounced decline in the South between 1968 and 1972 is attributable to the fact that some districts had only token desegregation as recently as 1968. Data for 1968 are from *Toward Equal Educational Opportunity,* The Report of the Select Committee on Equal Educational Opportunity, U. S. Senate Report No. 92-000 (Washington, D.C.: Gov-

ernment Printing Office, 1972), pp. 116–118. Source for 1970 and 1972 figures is reported in Table 3-2.

27. For example, in 1971 both Nashville, Tennessee, and Toledo, Ohio, had 27.2 percent black school systems. Between 1968 and 1971 the percentage of black students in schools having enrollments 80 to 100 percent black dropped from 64.1 to 0 percent in Nashville.

28. Quoted in *Toward Equal Educational Opportunity*, p. 311.

29. Kenneth B. Clark, *Dark Ghetto* (New York: Harper Torchbooks, 1965), p. 131. See pp. 139–148 for evidence on the beneficial effects of positive teacher attitudes. The need to reform the educational system to meet the needs of poor students, rather than discarding them as hopeless, is part of the problem discussed by William Ryan, *Blaming the Victim* (New York: Pantheon, 1971). Ryan argues that when we classify poor students as educationally unreachable, we blame them rather than society for the unpalatable product offered in many ghetto schools.

30. From interviews collected under National Science Foundation Grants GS-38157 and GS-38158 made to Charles S. Bullock, III and Harrell R. Rodgers, Jr.

31. *DeFunis* v. *Odegaard* .... U.S. .... (1974), questioned the constitutionality of law school admission procedures that accept minority students who have lower grades and aptitude scores than do whites who were rejected. The Supreme Court dismissed the case as moot. Plaintiff had been admitted to law school pursuant to a lower court order and was about to graduate. The Court of Appeals upheld the university.

32. Fredric B. Glantz and Nancy J. Delaney, "Changes in Nonwhite Residential Patterns in Large Metropolitan Areas, 1960–1970," *New England Economic Review* (March-April 1973), pp. 2–13.

33. *Toward Equal Educational Opportunity*, p. 120.

34. Calculations made from data in Annemette Sørensen, Karl E. Taeuber, and Leslie J. Hollingsworth, Jr., *Indexes of Racial Residential Segregation for 109 Cities in the United States, 1940 to 1970* (Madison, Wisc.: Institute for Research on Poverty, 1974), pp. 7–9.

35. Karl and Alma Taeuber, *Negroes in Cities* (Chicago: Aldine, 1965), pp. 35–36.

36. Lynn W. Eley and Thomas W. Casstevens, eds., *The Politics of Fair-Housing Legislation* (San Francisco: Chandler, 1968), p. xi.

37. For a discussion of state open-housing laws see Duane Lockard, *Toward Equal Opportunity* (London: Macmillan, 1968), pp. 102–133.

38. Data collected from U. S. Bureau of the Census, Census of Housing, 1970, *Metropolitan Housing Characteristics*, Final Report HC (2)-15, Atlanta, Georgia, SMSA (Washington, D.C.: Government Printing Office, 1972).

39. Karl Taeuber, "Residential Segregation," *Scientific American* (August 1965), pp. 17–18.

40. "Angry—But They Still Have a Dream," *Newsweek*, June 30, 1969, p. 20. The proportion of blacks preferring to live in biracial neighborhoods stood at 74 percent in 1969, up from 64 percent in 1963. Earlier

poll results are in William Brink and Louis Harris, *Black and White* (New York: Simon and Schuster, 1966), p. 232. Cf. Gary Marx, *Protest and Prejudice* (New York: Harper and Row, 1967), p. 224.

41. "Own-Choice Housing Hailed," *Atlanta Journal-Constitution,* July 9, 1972, p. 12-B.

42. U. S. Commission on Civil Rights, *One Year Later* (Washington, D.C.: Government Printing Office, 1971), p. 45.

43. *Toward Equal Educational Opportunity,* p. 122.

44. Between 1962 and 1967, 6.8 percent of FHA guaranteed housing went to minorities. U.S. Commission of Civil Rights, *Federal Civil Rights Enforcement Effort* (Washington, D.C.: Government Printing Office, 1970), pp. 491–492.

45. U.S. Department of Housing and Urban Affairs, *1971 HUD Statistical Yearbook* (Washington, D.C.: Government Printing Office, 1972), p. 130.

46. James L. Rowe, Jr., "Mortgage Rules Biased Against Minorities, Elderly, Women," *Washington Post,* October 5, 1971, p. A-6.

47. U.S. Commission on Civil Rights, *Federal Civil Rights Enforcement Effort,* p. 446.

48. "Growing Issue: Communities vs. Low-Income Housing," *Congressional Quarterly Weekly Report,* 30 (January 8, 1972), 54.

49. U. S. Commission on Civil Rights, *Federal Civil Rights Enforcement Effort—A Reassessment* (Washington, D.C.: Government Printing Office, 1973), p. 118.

50. *1971, HUD Statistical Yearbook,* p. 89.

51. *Ibid.;* and U.S. Commission on Civil Rights, *Federal Civil Rights Enforcement Effort,* pp. 448–454.

52. U.S. Commission on Civil Rights, *Federal Civil Rights Enforcement Effort,* pp. 159–186.

53. Haywood Burns, "Can a Black Man Get a Fair Trial in This Country," *New York Times Magazine,* July 12, 1970, reprinted in *Race, Creed, Color, or National Origin,* ed. Robert K. Yin (Itasca, Ill.: F. E. Peacock, 1973), p. 225.

54. Michael O. Finkelstein, "The Application of Statistical Decision Theory to the Jury Discrimination Cases," *Harvard Law Review,* 80 (December 1966), 338–376.

55. Jules B. Gerard and T. Rankin Terry, "Discrimination Against Negroes in the Administration of Criminal Law in Missouri," *Washington University Law Review* (Fall 1970), 436.

56. "City Vice Judge Thinks Justice Better for Blacks," *Atlanta Journal,* August 16, 1973, p. 20-A.

57. Figures taken from 1968, 1970, 1971, 1972, and 1973 volumes of the *National Roster of Black Elected Officials* (Washington, D.C.: Joint Center for Political Studies).

CHAPTER FOUR

Minority Groups and Welfare Goals

As status objectives have gradually been achieved, minorities have increasingly emphasized welfare goals. Economic disparities loom larger once progress toward political and social rights has been made, because some status gains cannot be fully utilized without economic improvement. For example, access to public accommodations and housing may be hollow to those unable to afford the prices. Moreover, because self-esteem is closely tied to economic success for most people, growing ethnic or racial pride resulting from status gains will produce greater emphasis on economic matters.

Various civil rights leaders have acknowledged the shift in emphasis from social to economic matters. For example, Vernon Jordan, executive director of the National Urban League, has said:

> [T]he goals of the March on Washington for Jobs and Freedom remain after a decade, as haunting reminders of ideas not yet fulfilled. . . . The freedoms envisioned by the March have largely been won. But freedom without economic power is freedom without substance. . . . We must get those jobs because economic security is a fundamental freedom from which other freedoms flow.[1]

In this chapter we deal with two broad types of programs to enhance the economic security of minorities. One facet will be programs aimed at improving job opportunities. This includes fair employment and manpower training activities. The other aspect is welfare programs for those not in the labor market.

The organization of this chapter parallels that of the two preceding ones. Actions against overt racism are discussed first, and then we look at steps taken against institutional racism. The effects of efforts directed at both types of discrimination are evaluated. Prospects for future federal actions are also reviewed. The chapter concludes with a brief discussion of the elements essential for public policy to succeed in achieving minority objectives in both status and welfare spheres.

OVERT RACISM

Many employers—private and public—have traditionally refused to hire minorities for any but menial chores. When minorities were hired for nonmenial tasks (for example, as black teachers in the South), they were often paid less than whites. Denial of access to better positions forced minorities to take jobs whites did not want. The hottest, the dirtiest, the smelliest, the poorest paying tasks were reserved for nonwhites. Labor unions often barred minorities from apprenticeship programs, or relegated them to separate occupations—for example, as railroad porters.

In defining acceptable behavior in the economic sphere, the benchmark used to measure progress has been the proportion of minority workers in various jobs. The policy objective is for minorities to be approximately equally distributed throughout the labor force.

The initial federal acknowledgment that minorities were entitled to equal employment opportunities came in the early 1940s. As America geared up to supply the wartime needs of the allies, A. Philip Randolph, president of the Brotherhood of Sleeping Car Porters, threatened a March on Washington to protest job discrimination. To avert this disruption, President

Roosevelt issued an executive order prohibiting discrimination by military suppliers. (Ironically, although defense contractors were called on to cease discrimination, the Armed Forces maintained segregated units throughout World War II.) The Fair Employment Practices Committee (FEPC) was created to handle complaints but restricted its activities to attempts at resolving difficulties through voluntary efforts. Once the war was won, the FEPC was allowed to die.

Between 1963 and 1965 the United States government, after almost two decades of dereliction, again acknowledged responsibility for protecting minority employment rights. Executive orders from Presidents Kennedy and Johnson established equal employment programs in federal agencies and for firms receiving federal contracts. Title VII of the 1964 Civil Rights Act forbade discrimination by private businesses, unions, and employment agencies having twenty-five or more workers. New agencies were created and charged with overseeing fair employment efforts: the Office of Federal Contract Compliance (OFCC), responsible for federal contractors, and the Equal Employment Opportunity Commission (EEOC), responsible for private businesses and unions generally. The Civil Service Commission (CSC) was designated to lead in efforts within the federal government. The edicts establishing these rights provided for active federal involvement. However, as our analysis shows, agencies entrusted with enforcement have often defaulted.

Establishing Standards

Programs in the private sector have, from their inception, acknowledged the need for affirmative action. For example, the EEOC proudly stated in its *Second Annual Report*: "Recognizing that complaints are an insufficient measure of the extent to which job discrimination exists, the Commission strove ... to transcend the case-by-case compliance process and stimulate the kinds of broad scale affirmative action by the employment community which would combat the effects of past and present racism."[2] Affirmative action has, at a minimum, required that employers agree to launch programs that will expand minority representation throughout the range of job categories. Often, however, the enforcement agencies have accepted nebulous commitments from employers. For example, CSC has not only permitted federal agencies to file proposals that are so vague as to defy subsequent evaluation; it has also allowed the filing of plans that had already proven ineffective.[3]

Imprecise proposals are characteristic of the tendency of compliance agencies to view affirmative action largely as a voluntary matter. Rather than *imposing* standards, agencies have preferred to work with employers in developing techniques to increase minority participation. Thus, until recently CSC offered its services to other federal agencies rather than requiring submission of goals and timetables. EEOC has, on request of employers, participated in devising affirmative action plans. Failure to act more aggressively is rationalized in the EEOC assertion that "it takes more than bureaucrats and judges to end centuries of discrimination in employment. Only the *voluntary compliance* of an informed American industry can do that."[4] Voluntary acceptance is indeed important, but experience shows that it cannot be relied on exclusively.

Only slowly have the three agencies promulgated standards. Not until 1971 did CSC acknowledge that goals and timetables could be useful in evaluating progress.[5] It still has not established standards for judging internal upward mobility efforts. OFCC did not specify its expectations as to the number of contracts that should be reviewed annually until 1969, and then waited more than a year before providing guidelines for evaluation. EEOC, while diverting a quarter of the complaints it received to the fair employment practices commissions of the states in which the complaints originated, did not set standards for state commissions until 1971. In the meantime numerous complaints suffered unnecessary delays while EEOC deferred action for sixty days, awaiting the outcome of state procedures that had already proven ineffective. In the slipshod early days, some complaints were denied relief altogether because of procedural confusion.

The most promising use of standards appears to occur when numerical objectives are established that are to be met within a specified time period. OFCC instituted some of the earliest specific plans. Beginning in Philadelphia, plans have been developed for achieving approximately the same proportion of minority workers in the lucrative construction trades as in the local labor force. By 1973 plans had been drawn up for fifty-four urban areas. Court orders and consent decrees have also established minimal goals for public employers to meet in hiring minority workers.[6]

Complaint Processing

The tardiness and imprecision that had characterized the issuance of standards is partially caused by the greater emphasis given complaints. This is particularly true of EEOC, which during its first seven years received more than 110,000 allegations of discrimination. Although race or ethnicity is not the only basis for complaints, it accounts for approximately two-thirds of them. In fiscal year 1970, 70 percent of EEOC's manpower was involved in resolving complaints.[7]

Complaint processing is insufficient when it is the primary activity of an enforcement agency, rather than simply a remedial tool. The chief deficiency is, of course, the narrower impact inherent in a case-by-case approach. Despite its inefficiency, complaint processing can help define the limits of acceptable behavior. EEOC decisions have established, for example, that employers cannot rely on word-of-mouth recruiting but must pursue channels likely to reach minorities—such as advertising in minority papers. An important advance has been the commission's willingness to rely on statistical evidence to create a rebuttable presumption of discrimination. For example, if an employer's share of minority employees is much smaller than the proportion in the area's labor force, it is assumed that this is the product of past or present discrimination, even if prejudice cannot be documented. The burden is on the employer to demonstrate the absence of discrimination.

EEOC complaint processing has been fraught with problems. Despite the emphasis placed on this activity, the backlog swelled to more than 50,000 cases by 1972, and delays of two years are common. Every step of the process is slow and the likelihood that the complainant will win is small. Of 41,000 investigations conducted during its first seven years, conciliations were undertaken in 9,188 cases, of which 2,501 were successfully resolved. Thus, only 2 percent of all complaints received were favorably acted on by the EEOC, despite an estimate by one commission chairman that 80 percent of the complaints were justified.[8] Complaints have often been dealt with narrowly, with no attempt to expand the inquiry into a class action, or to check for types of discrimination other than those cited in the complaint. Finally, the enforcement powers granted the commission by the 1964 Act restricted it to the voluntary tactics of conference, conciliation, and persuasion.

Litigation

During the period when EEOC was restricted to voluntary efforts, there was the potential for referring unresolved charges to the Justice Department for prosecution. This remedy was not commonly resorted to despite EEOC's low success rate. By the end of fiscal 1972 EEOC had sent 239 cases to the Attorney General, but relatively few suits had been filed pursuant to these referrals. Poor Justice follow-through is partially attributable to shoddy investigative work and slowness by EEOC, which caused files to become dated or cases to become moot.

Litigation by Justice produced decisions that added legitimacy and the weight of legal precedent to the efforts of compliance agencies to negotiate settlements. The role of the Justice Department should diminish in the wake of 1972 legislation that authorizes EEOC to institute litigation. Henceforth, when defendants balk at commission conciliatory efforts, EEOC can seek judicial enforcement without having to await a suit by the Attorney General.

A second judicial recourse available to complainants has been private litigation. In the past, if EEOC persuasion failed, the complainant could use EEOC recommendations as the basis for a suit. The Commission has participated in several hundred private actions as *amicus curiae*. Frequently judges have relied heavily on EEOC proposals in granting relief.

Monitoring Compliance

All three compliance agencies have taken the first step toward efficient monitoring. Data are collected on the number of minority workers in various occupational categories. Insufficient research has been done to determine the extent to which these data are used to measure progress or to direct enforcement efforts.

When a compliance agency sets out to monitor progress and is willing to use its sanctioning powers, substantial advances can be achieved. The persistence needed to obtain large increases in minority employment is well illustrated by OFCC experiences in Philadelphia. The second-year goal for minority employment in the construction industry in that city was met, but only after issuance of more than one hundred show cause orders threatening contract termination and one disbarment.[9] Usually compliance agencies do not display such tenacity. Generally they are understaffed and undermotivated.

INSTITUTIONAL RACISM

Minority employment has been particularly susceptible to institutional racism. Employment prerequisites often require attributes that minorities are less likely to have than whites. A second disadvantage which results from past discrimination, is a proportionally larger absence of marketable skills among minorities.

Employment Prerequisites

Courts and compliance agencies have questioned a number of traditional conditions for employment. Unless an employer can demonstrate that the job prerequisites that he imposes are indeed predictors of job performance, he must discontinue them if they disproportionately exclude minorities. This approach has led to proscription of such requirements as a high school education and no record of arrests or convictions. Employers are also responsible for validating the employment tests they use. "Thus, where a test has a disparate effect on minority groups, the employer has the burden of demonstrating ... both that the tests it has been using are accurate and useful predictors of performance in each of the jobs for which they are prerequisites and that reasonable alternate employee selection techniques do not exist."[10] Ironically, while private employers have had their tests validated, the Federal Service Entrance Examination—which is used for more than two hundred job categories—has not been validated.

Use of seniority systems is also forbidden if they perpetuate past discrimination. To count seniority earned by whites during a time in which minorities were denied jobs serves to freeze the racist practices of the past. Nor can minority workers be forced to give up seniority in order to take what had been white jobs in companies that had segregated seniority rosters.

Employment Skills

Even if prerequisites and written tests that are unrelated to job performance are abolished and valid skills tests are substituted, people who are prepared only for low skill jobs will still face an insurmountable wall of institutional racism. Technological advances reduce opportunities for those lacking skills. During periods of low unemployment, private industry voluntarily provides training for some workers. In times of high unemployment there is an adequate supply of available labor and manpower training, if it is provided, must be publicly financed.

During the 1960s, a number of manpower programs were developed. Some were directed toward specific groups—for example, Job Corps and Neighborhood Youth Corps (NYC) for teenagers and young adults. The Work Incentive Program (WIN) was targeted for welfare recipients, and Operation Mainstream served chronically unemployed heads of families.[11]

The various programs are of two types. Some are structured preparatory training for specific jobs. The training may consist of on-the-job experience or classroom instruction. Manpower Development and Training (MDTA), Job Corps, and the privately operated Job Opportunities in the Business Sector (JOBS) are programs which teach skills. The second and larger aspect of manpower training is work experience programs. People who are unaccustomed to the behavioral expectations associated with regular job-holding are taught grooming and job etiquette and offered counseling. Participants are placed in low skill jobs as an introduction to the world of work. Sometimes these jobs are created by federal subsidies offered to public or private employers. New Careers and the Public Employment Program (PEP) offer money to public agencies that will employ the jobless. WIN and NYC are also work experience programs, but many of their enrollees are hired by private concerns that have some of their costs reimbursed by the federal government.

Minority participation in manpower programs varies, although in all such programs minorities constitute a larger proportion than in the population generally. In fiscal 1973, minorities comprised the largest proportion of the Job Corps (75.3 percent) and were least often found in MDTA-OJT (41.3 percent). Minorities constituted 52.2 percent of the generally more effective, structured training programs in fiscal 1973.

Employment Opportunities in Black Business

In a third area, programs seek to expand minority employment opportunities by offsetting institutionally racist financing restrictions facing minority businessmen. The anticipated employment payoff rests on the assumption that minority businessmen will more readily hire minority workers than will whites. The best known program is black capitalism. However, minorities in general qualify for several forms of assistance. Minority businessmen can obtain federal loans up to $25,000 from the Small Business Administration, 90 percent federal guarantees on bank loans, expert advice, and noncompetitive contracts for goods and services from federal agencies.[12] Presently the Office of Minority Business Enterprise is emphasizing aid to existing concerns and is encouraging minority businessmen to purchase franchises in national chains rather than to go out on their own.[13]

A number of blacks reject the appropriateness of the capitalist model to meet black needs.[14] They fear that even if capitalism were grafted onto the ghetto economy, it would provide few benefits for the masses. Alternative proposals have suggested the development of cooperatives. The Congress on Racial Equality helped draft legislation that would create Community Development Corporations run by blacks in major cities. Legislation provided for community development banks and a financing plan modeled on the Farm Credit System. Each CDC would operate a variety of businesses. Some of the profits would be spent for community improvements, such as day-care facilities and drug clinics.

Implementation of both black capitalism and the CDC proposal has lagged. Enabling legislation for CDCs never passed Congress, although a few have been funded through the Office of Economic Opportunity. Black capitalism and other programs have never been fleshed out financially. A book-length study of Nixon's black capitalism program concludes that, "It was a mockery of the President's own vow to give them [blacks] 'a piece of the action.' "[15] Blaustein and Faux fault the Nixon Administration for both poor faith and poor ideas. The cabinet member responsible for black capitalism, Commerce Secretary Stans, abjured specific goals, institutional change, and large-scale resource commitment. Moreover, the authors charge the administration with embracing the wrong model. Black capitalism focused on developing small "mom and pop" businesses, risky undertakings in which the failure rate approaches 80 percent and which—even if they succeed—provide few jobs. Finally, the funds provided for minority businesses have been insufficient for success.

EVALUATION

Equal Employment Opportunities

The trends of recent years are clear. In both private and public employment there has been an increase in the number of minority workers in the better job categories. Data on federal employment in Table 4-1 show minority representation in all sets of grades increasing between 1965 and 1972, with the proportion of General Schedule positions filled by minorities up from 11.1 to 15.1 percent. The format of this table is such that a ratio of 1.00 indicates that minorities comprise the same proportion of a particular occupation as they do of the larger labor force (for example, 15.1 percent in 1972). Ratios below 1.00 indicate minority underrepresentation, and scores above 1.00 indicate that minorities are disproportionately found in the occupation. Minority overrepresentation in the lowest ranks has declined since 1969. Although underrepresentation continues above grade GS 9, the situation continues to improve, particularly at top grades above GS 14.

Table 4-2 reports improvements in the status of minority workers in the private sector where minorities now comprise 15.3 percent of the labor force, up from 10.9 percent in 1966. Between 1966 and 1973, minorities were increasingly repre-

TABLE 4-1

Minority Employment in General Schedule Jobs of the Federal Government[a]

Grade	1965[b]	1969	1972
Overall Proportion Minority	*11.1%*	*13.2%*	*15.1%*
GS 1–4	1.98	1.98	1.83
GS 5–8	1.03	1.21	1.15
GS 9–11	.40	.53	.57
GS 12–13		.27	.31
GS 14–15	.14	.18	.25
GS 16–18		.12	.22

[a] Ratios computed on distribution of minority workers per occupation to distribution expected if minorities constituted the same proportion of all occupations.

[b] 1965 data slightly underrepresent the presence of all minorities other than blacks.

Sources: U.S. Civil Service Commission, *Study of Minority Group Employment in the Federal Government* (Washington, D.C.: Government Printing Office, 1967, 1969, and 1972).

sented in all white-collar categories and among craftsmen and operatives. Although the lowest categories—laborers and service workers—still have uncommonly large numbers of minorities, both registered a shift toward equalization. While all minority groups have experienced improvement, blacks remain generally less equitably distributed across occupatioins than either Hispanics or American Indians.[16] If one looks at all people currently working, rather than only at the larger firms for which data are reported in Table 4-2, the proportion of nonwhites in white-collar jobs is substantially higher, standing at .68 in 1973.[17] This suggests a more frequent representation of minorities in government (in 1973, minorities constituted 20.4 percent of federal employees[18] and 15.3 percent of larger private firms) and in smaller businesses.

TABLE 4-2

Minority Employment in Firms Having 100 or More Employees[a]

Occupation	1966	1973
White collar	.36	.54
Professional	.20	.31
Technical	.52	.68
Managers and officials	.15	.29
Sales	.37	.52
Clerical	.48	.78
Blue collar	1.33	1.31
Craftsmen	.53	.69
Operatives	1.29	1.39
Laborers	2.54	2.01
Service	2.51	2.05
Overall Proportion Minority	10.9%	15.3%

[a] Ratios computed on distribution of minority workers per occupation to distribution expected if minorities constituted the same proportion of all occupations.

Source: Computed from data in Department of Labor, *Manpower Report of the President* (Washington, D.C.: Government Printing Office, 1974), pp. 383–384.

The broad occupational categories hide some variation. What Moore has observed among Mexican Americans is applicable to other minorities. "Mexicans hold the poorer jobs inside broad occupational classifications. Professional and technical job holders, for example, are far more likely to be medical social workers than lawyers. In the managerial classification there are far more managers of small marginal restaurants than corporate executives."[19] Equally as clear as the improvements registered are the discrepancies between minority representation in job categories and minority presence in the labor force. Despite recent gains, minorities remain substantially underrepresented in better-paying jobs. Gaps are particularly large at the highest levels, professional and managerial positions and federal supergrades. (In 1972 minorities had only 22 percent of the GS 16 through 18 slots that their numbers would have justified.) Unless the rate of progress greatly increases, it will take a long time to correct minority underrepresentation in the better jobs.

Although there are grounds for criticizing efforts to increase minority presence in better jobs, the complicity of the educational system and society at large must not be overlooked. Racism long excluded minorities from most professional schools. Racism also infected the quality of education and training offered many minority students in racially isolated public schools. Consequently, the supply of appropriately trained minorities is inadequate in a number of occupations.

Manpower Programs

The success of manpower training varies by program; however, structured job training generally receives higher marks than does work experience.[20] Minorities who have received on-the-job training (OJT) earn higher wages than do those who have been through work experience projects.[21] In fiscal 1973, black MDTA-OJT completers averaged $3.60 per hour while Spanish-speaking completers averaged $4.11. At the other end of the scale, black and Spanish-speaking graduates of Comprehensive Employment Programs which have a work experience orientation, averaged $2.33 and $2.43 an hour, respectively.

In the past, employment rates have also been appreciably higher for terminators of structured job training than for other programs. In fiscal 1972, employment rates for the former ranged from 48 to 80 percent while for the latter the range was 30 to 45 percent.[22] Data for fiscal 1973 suggest some narrowing of the difference in job placements for the two types of manpower programs. While two skill programs—Job Corps and MDTA-OJT—had the highest post-program employment rates

(78 percent), two work experience programs had higher placements than did two other skill programs.[23] It should be noted, however, that even completers of the most successful programs experienced 22 percent unemployment.

Work experience programs are generally less desirable than OJT because they "consistently fail to impart a sense of the importance of production. Actually, the lack of useful work experience is probably best explained by the observation that neither administrators nor enrollees appear to consider the work stations as real jobs."[24] Given the greater success of structured training, it is ironic that in fiscal 1973 only 24 percent of the enrollees and 23 percent of the manpower budget went to these types of program.

Lack of emphasis on structured training raises questions about the goals of manpower program administrators. There is evidence that the chief objective may be to process as many people as possible rather than to insure that enrollees get jobs. Programs are usually structured so that participants are enrolled too briefly to acquire anything beyond low-level skills. This has prompted the comment that: "In a significant way, we trained blacks to move from unskilled unemployment to various shades of skilled unemployment and underemployment."[25] This criticism alludes to yet another defect: the preparation of enrollees for jobs that do not exist.

Manpower programs have often failed to meet the needs of prospective clients. People with severe or multiple problems have often been ignored, especially by skill training programs. There is some question whether skill training programs do anything more than subsidize employers for activities they would have performed without the program. Critics have charged of MDTA-OJT that it "has never been able to prove conclusively that its trainees were any different in characteristics and needs from those the employer would have *hired* in the absence of any subsidy."[26] Furthermore, high dropout rates from some programs suggest their failure to meet the needs of enrollees. Rather than shrugging off dropouts as the product of low enrollee motivation, programs should be restructured to better serve the needs of enrollees.

Finally, although many minorities continue to badly need manpower training, their presence in the skill training programs has declined. Nonwhite enrollment in the institutional aspect of MDTA peaked in fiscal 1968 and in the OJT aspect the following year. Minority participation in the federally financed portion of JOBS has dropped since fiscal 1969. As the economy has cooled and unemployment has risen, whites have increasingly replaced minorities in the more successful programs. By fiscal 1973, there was a perfect inverse correlation between the proportion of blacks in a program and the average earnings of program completers.[27]

Unemployment Rates

One measure of the impact of equal employment and manpower programs is the rate of unemployment. If minority employment goals are being met, then minority unemployment rates should become increasingly similar to those of whites. On this score, the record is poor. In all but two years since 1954, the unemployment rate for nonwhites has been at least twice as great as for whites. The minimum occurred in 1970 and 1971, when nonwhites were 1.8 times as likely to be out of work as whites. By 1973, the ratio had risen to 2.1:1, but with a slight improvement registered in mid-1974.

The lowest nonwhite unemployment rate in recent years was 6.4 percent in 1969. Thus, even when there is relatively full employment among whites (white unemployment was 3.1 percent in 1969), unemployment remains at recession levels among nonwhites. In September 1974, the rates for whites and nonwhites were 5.2 and 9.7 percent respectively. Among teenage nonwhites, the unemployment rate was above 30 percent from 1971 to 1973. Dismal as these statistics are, they do not give the full picture. When jobs are hard to find, some people cease trying and drop out of the labor force. It has been estimated that if these dropouts were included, unemployment rates would double.[28]

Unemployment rates for other minorities also exceed those of whites. Latest available figures show 7.5 percent unemployment among workers of Spanish origin in 1973 and 11.6 percent unemployment among American Indians in 1970.[29] Manpower training and the spread of fair employment opportunities have not altered the two-decade-old relationship between white and minority unemployment.

Income

Success of manpower and equal employment opportunity programs might bring about a reduction in the gap between white and minority incomes. Between 1960 and 1973, the median family income for nonwhite families more than doubled, from $3,233 to $7,596.[30] The rate of growth, however, was only slightly better than that of white families, whose median income rose from $5,835 to $12,595. The ratio of nonwhite to white incomes rose from .53 in 1963 to .64 in 1970. But by 1973, as the economy cooled, the relative position of nonwhites had deteriorated, and their median income dropped to .60 of the white figure. Nonwhites in the West are best off, earning 81 percent as much as whites, while in the South they earned only 56 percent as much. These data show that even though some minority families are doing much better now than in the past and the number of middle-class minority members is growing, the overall relative position of nonwhites has improved very little.[31] Moreover, the current rate of progress is insufficient to close the gap between black and white incomes rapidly.

WELFARE PROGRAMS

One reason for the persisting income gap between whites and minorities is that a larger share of the latter are unable to earn an adequate wage. Many of these people are outside the labor force; they are too old, too young, handicapped, or have too many dependents. Many minorities rely on categoric assistance and other welfare programs for what little they have.

Minorities disproportionately receive some form of public assistance. In 1971, 25 percent of all black families, compared with 5 percent of whites, received public assistance.[32] Blacks accounted for 38 percent of all welfare recipients. In the largest and least popular welfare program, Aid to Families with Dependent Children (AFDC), blacks constituted 42 percent of the recipients.[33]

Welfare assistance is of two types. Categoric assistance (AFDC and Supplemental Security Income) expands the purchasing power of the poor, usually by giving them money. Public housing provides a good, either free of charge or at less than market value.

Despite the differences in types of programs, both sets are susceptible to the same kinds of criticism. First, they do not serve all of the needy, as evidenced by waiting lists for public housing. Second, because states fix the level of benefits for AFDC, there is a wide range.[34] In 1971, direct welfare payments varied from a low of $60 a month for a family of four in Mississippi to $372 per month in Alaska.[35] Third, the programs often operate in an adversary relationship to their clients, with administrators trying to limit participation. One critic has charged that "The welfare system is designed to save money instead of people and tragically ends up doing neither."[36] Fourth, the stereotypic suspicion that the plight of the poor is caused by their own indolence and immorality has led to narrow definitions of eligibility. Many states have not yet accepted the AFDC option that allows payments to families in which the father is unable to find work. This myopia permits a deserted family to qualify for benefits while one having an unemployed father does not—thus producing incentive for desertion. Fifth, benefits—rather than declining gradually as the recipient's economic position improves—are often terminated abruptly when one has even a meager income. The loss of subsidized public housing or welfare payments may more than offset what one might earn, and thus incentive is stifled.

A widely discussed remedy that would meet the above criticisms is the negative income tax, of which Nixon's Family Assistance Plan was one version.[37] The negative income tax, which is under consideration by the Ford Administration, would give poor people a minimum income. As recipients' earnings increase, their federal benefits are reduced by a proportionate amount. For example, for each two dollars earned, the amount of Negative Income Tax received might drop one dollar. Illustrative figures in Table 4-3 show that the program builds in a work incentive, because the more one earns, the greater his total disposable income. Thus, a family of four might receive a minimum of $900 per person, or $3,600. A four-person family that earned $1,500 would have that amount plus $2,850 Negative Income Tax. Other minimal figures and rates for phasing out benefits have, of course, been proposed.

TABLE 4-3

Total Disposable Income of a Family of Four Under a Negative Income Tax Plan Which Pays $900 per Person and is Reduced by $1 for Every $2 Earned

Earnings	$ 0	$1,000	$1,500	$3,000	$5,500	$7,200
Negative income tax	3,600	3,100	2,850	2,100	850	0
Total	$3,600	$4,100	$4,350	$5,100	$6,350	$7,200

PROSPECTS FOR THE FUTURE

Currently equal employment opportunities are the aspect of minority welfare goals that seem most likely to be realized, although distributions, particularly among top jobs, will not become fully equalized for some time. For example, a recent study of employment practices in Atlanta concluded that "there was no overt evidence of deliberate efforts to exclude minority applicants from employment."[38] Although the researchers did find instances of institutional racism, they noted a number of activities designed to overcome such problems—for example, recruiting efforts at minority schools, company awareness of equal opportunity responsibilities, less reliance on written tests, and the use of tests validated as free of discrimination. Minority workers who are qualified seem no longer to be denied good jobs.

New legislative authority has coincided with changes in employer attitudes and behavior. Legislation of 1972 expanded EEOC and CSC authority and seems to have encouraged these agencies to become more aggressive. EEOC can enforce its compliance decisions by seeking court orders rather than awaiting action by the Justice Department. The Commission has also improved its relations with state and local fair employment practices committees. This should reduce EEOC's workload and expedite decisions without impairing the rights of complainants. In 1974, EEOC achieved a major breakthrough, negotiating a detailed affirmative action plan that sets goals and timetables for minority employment for an entire industry, steel. Previous affirmative action plans have been limited to single installations or individual companies.

A 1974 settlement negotiated between the Bank of America and its women employees suggests another potential technique for overcoming the effects of racism. Under this unique agreement, the Bank of America will set aside a $3.75 million trust fund to finance training, education, and other self-improvement programs for its female workers.[39] Minorities may well demand similar programs in the future.

CSC has become more demanding, recognizing the value of goals and timetables for federal agencies. Agencies must now file annual affirmative action plans, which CSC seems to be evaluating more carefully.[40] Minority representation in the federal government continues to grow albeit at a slower rate, even as the size of the federal work force is reduced.

Manpower training has also undergone recent change, but it is still unclear to what extent minorities are likely to benefit. The Comprehensive Employment and Training Act (CETA) of 1973 is a revenue sharing bill. It eliminated many of the manpower programs, consolidating them into a smaller number of budgetary categories. Federal control will be reduced, and most money will go directly to state and local governments, which will have wide latitude in the types of manpower training to be offered. It is problematic whether state and local authorities will emphasize programs to impart skills or instead will fund work experience programs. What is certain is that, regardless of the mix of programs undertaken, the funding available will decline. The CETA budget is not scheduled to grow fast enough to keep pace with inflation. The burden of declining budgets will fall heavily on the needy. "Programs for the poor, the unemployed, and underemployed served by CETA are slated for the sharpest cuts."[41] As noted, one weakness of manpower training has been that training has been too brief to prepare people for most jobs that pay well. The smaller purchasing power of CETA budgets may lead to a further reduction in program lengths. This bodes ill for people rendered jobless because of multiple problems.

Even if there was more generous funding, some would question the desirability of granting broad leeway to state and local officials. Several black spokesmen are critical of revenue sharing. Vernon Jordan has cautioned, "The effect of revenue sharing on white people is likely to be harmful; for black people, it promises to be devastating."[42] Congressman Andrew Young (D-Georgia) castigates revenue sharing, charging that:

> To black Americans, who historically had no choice but to look to the federal government to correct the abuses of state and local governments, that is very much like hiring the wolf to guard the sheep. It is axiomatic in American political life, with some exceptions, that the lower the level of government,

the lower the level of competence and the higher the margin of discrimination against the poor and the powerless.[43]

Indians and Spanish-speaking people will be less dependent on local administrators because some CETA money is earmarked for them.

A problem that seems unlikely to be remedied in the near future is high minority unemployment. Although the idea that the federal government should guarantee jobs to all who are seeking work has been around a long time, there is no indication that it is close to implementation. A short step in this direction was the 1971 Emergency Employment Act, which created 150,000 public service jobs for each of the next two years. This small program was more a gesture than a serious commitment to stanch unemployment. The program has been continued under CETA, but funding has been cut and eligibility requirements have been raised. The program was reduced in the face of predictions now borne out, of rising unemployment during 1974.

The last of the items discussed in the context of minority status goals was welfare. Some reforms have already been implemented. Beginning in 1974, the federal government assumed responsibility for the aged, blind, and disabled. This introduced uniformity of payments in an area previously marked by wide differences under a federal-state matching relationship. One would hope for revamping AFDC, perhaps institution of a negative income tax or some other program that would cure the current defects. If this is not achieved, perhaps reasonable minimal standards will be imposed on states.

CORRELATES OF PROGRESS

Despite variation in the extent to which racism has been corrected, changes have occurred in each policy area considered in the last three chapters. We conclude this chapter by noting briefly some of the correlates of change in civil rights. This analysis sheds light on the reasons for the differing amounts of progress observed.

The fundamental reason that greater progress has not been made is, of course, the widespread opposition of many of the whites most likely to be affected by changed race relations. As already pointed out, a number of whites derive benefits from subordinating minorities, and most whites do not understand how racism functions. Naturally, many of those who enjoy the status quo tenaciously resist attempts at change.

Precision of Requirements

When civil rights laws are unpopular, the government must be prepared to achieve compliance through coercion, if necessary. In order to move forcefully against the noncompliant, the law must clearly define the behavior expected.

The most explicit requirements have been set for voter registration and the desegregation of *de jure* school systems. Literacy tests have been banned nationwide, and other tests and devices are inappropriate prerequisites for registration in a numerically defined set of states and counties (i.e. those in which less than half of the voting age population was registered or voted in 1968). The law requires that school districts once guilty of *de jure* segregation have approximately the same racial composition in each school's faculty and, while somewhat more variance is tolerated, are to eliminate racially identifiable schools. Use of numerical standards or goals and the specific prohibition on some actions facilitate identification of the noncompliant. These are much more precise standards than the simple prohibition of discrimination found in *Brown*, the 1957 and 1968 Civil Rights Acts, and *Norris* or *Hernandez*.[44]

The more recent standards in voting and education have redefined what must be done, making token minority participation no longer sufficient. For example, freedom-of-choice plans for school desegregation are no longer adequate unless they eliminate racially identifiable schools.

Severity of Sanctions

A second requirement for progress is that there be meaningful sanctions and that noncompliance evoke sure and swift punishment. For example, a study in progress, on the implementation of school desegregation in a sample of Georgia schools, is uncovering evidence that dual schools were eliminated in many districts only after local authorities believed that state funds might be enjoined and that they would be held personally liable for their districts' noncompliance.[45] Once the federal government demonstrated that it would compel full desegregation in a district, neighboring ones often "voluntarily" complied. In contrast, tools available to disperse low and moderate income housing (for example, refusal to fund HUD programs in communities lacking adequate housing opportunities for minorities and families of modest means) have not been utilized, and so such sanctions are not a credible threat. HUD actions have often contradicted the stated objectives of the laws, and housing programs are still typically operated on a segregated basis.

The consistency with which federal authorities deal with racism may be affected by the locus of monitoring and sanctioning responsibilities. In voting, employment, and education, the agency authorized to monitor progress is empowered to initiate actions against the noncompliant. The Department of Justice's Voting and Public Accommodations Section is responsible for voting activities, EEOC for employment, and OCR for schools. In contrast, HUD lacks coercive powers because it is limited to "conference, conciliation, and persuasion." When conciliation cannot be achieved, HUD must refer matters to the Department of Justice rather than seeking judicial or administrative enforcement on its own. The difficulty resulting from this division of responsibility can be illustrated using 1971 statistics on conciliations. Of 351 attempts that were concluded, 42 percent were unsuccessful—yet only 15 cases were referred to Justice.[46]

Legislative Involvement

Although courts can set standards as rigorous as those set by a legislature, courts may be more restricted in their ability to stimulate widespread change. Court decisions, like legislative acts, can establish the existence of a right. Unless the right is generally accepted, the declaration of its existence may be widely ignored. Thus, *Brown* was almost wholly ignored for years in the South. Many school systems continue to have morning devotions, and police extract confessions in violation of constitutional prohibitions.[47] In the absence of court monitoring (which is uncommon) or new litigation, violations will go uncorrected.

Legislative efforts may meet with similar evasions, but an important difference exists. Except for the litigants of a case—who, if they persist in proscribed behavior, are subject to contempt citations—court orders can be enforced on other noncompliant entities only through additional suits. For example, the *Brown* decision, while succeeding in opening white schools to blacks in the border states, was not acted on in many southern districts until they lost suits brought by local black parents or were subjected to some other pressures toward compliance. In some districts where no black parents sued the school board, *de jure* segregation continued undiluted until 1970.

Legislatures can authorize administrative agencies to carry out objectives. Congress directed HEW to achieve desegregation of public education facilities from kindergarten through college. Justice can act in voting and public accommodations, and EEOC is responsible for promoting equal employment opportunities. The agency responsible for enforcement may default, but that is a problem to be handled by Congress through administrative oversight or internally by the agency's superiors. What should be recognized is that courts lack the authority of a legislature to create an agency responsible for seeking out and acting against discrimination. Congressional authorization of agencies to pursue racism at least gives rise to the potential for more universal enforcement than is likely when litigation is the only recourse.

Burden of Proof

For a plaintiff to prevail in court, he must prove his allegations with a preponderance of evidence in a civil case and beyond a reasonable doubt in a criminal case. In the past plaintiffs alleging discrimination because of race had to prove that different treatment was accorded whites and blacks. Evidence of the underrepresentation of blacks on voting lists or in schools was often insufficient to sustain a finding of discrimination in the absence of a showing of white intent to exclude blacks. Obtuseness on the part of judges sometimes made such showings difficult. For example, some judges decided that the absence of black voters in counties with large black populations resulted not from discrimination but from lack of interest.[48]

Realization of minority rights has been facilitated whenever designated conditions have been held to create a presumption of discrimination, thereby obviating the need for minorities to offer proof. Standards of this type have been set in voting, *de jure* segregation, and employment.

The research has not yet been done that will permit assessment of the relative importance of the factors discussed above in achieving compliance. Each one no doubt plays some role. The success of public policy in changing racist behavior may well depend on both the number of components and on the rigor of the design of each component that is present.

SUMMARY

Two things have been done in this chapter. First, we analyzed programs which have helped minorities achieve welfare objectives. Welfare goals have involved demands for equal employment guarantees, expanded employment opportunities and adequate economic support for people outside the labor force. Although progress in the economic sphere, as in the status sphere, remains incomplete, obvious gains are being made. Minorities are obtaining a larger share of society's better jobs. And while the final evidence is not in on the effectiveness of manpower programs, they improve the earning abilities of some minority families.

Since there remains substantial room for improving economic programs, it is encouraging that in this area (more than in any other which we consider) public policy is still evolving. Since 1972 new legislation has been enacted which has affected each of the three policy components subsumed under welfare objectives. As standards and programs continue to develop, a number of the deficiencies noted in this chapter may be remedied. The increasingly strident demands of women may combine with minority demands to force improved federal policies for fair employment, manpower training, and welfare.

To some extent, however, minority attainment of full economic equality is contingent upon a complex mix of factors. Minorities are still too often the last hired and first fired. Therefore when the economy is sluggish, minorities are particularly hard hit. A return of the prosperity of the 1960s would create demands for workers which would draw more minorities into better paying jobs. A strong economy would also provide privately financed training opportunities for the unskilled and jobs for people who complete manpower programs.

In addition to dependence on the state of the economy, attainment of minority welfare objectives is partially a product of our educational and health delivery systems. There are minority adults who, because they were unable to afford health care or because they were given shockingly inadequate educations, are unable to compete in today's labor market. Some of these people are so ill-prepared that even outstanding manpower programs could not salvage them.

Second, we briefly summarized the evidence in Chapters 2 through 4 on the factors which have been associated with minority progress. Looking at both status and welfare objectives, advances have been greatest when the law establishes precise standards of acceptable behavior, threatens severe sanctions for noncompliance, provides for administrative as well as judicial enforcement, and shifts the legal burden of proof from minorities seeking to gain access to a right to those who would deny minority rights.

NOTES

1. Keynote address by Vernon E. Jordan, Jr., to the Sixty-third Annual Conference of the National Urban League, reprinted in the *Congressional Record,* 93rd Congress, 1st Session, 119 (August 1, 1973), p. E 5283.

2. Equal Employment Opportunity Commission, *Second Annual Report* (Washington, D.C.: Government Printing Office, 1968), p. 3.

3. U. S. Commission on Civil Rights, *Federal Civil Rights Enforcement Effort—A Reassessment* (Washington, D.C.: Government Printing Office, 1973), pp. 43–51.

4. Equal Employment Opportunity Commission, *Seventh Annual Report* (Washington, D.C.: Government Printing Office, 1973), p. 11, emphasis added.

5. For discussion of why the Civil Service Commission altered its policy, see David H. Rosenbloom, "The Civil Service Commission's Decision to Authorize the Use of Goals and Timetables in the Federal Equal Employment Opportunity Program," *Western Political Quarterly* 21 (June 1973), 236–251.

6. "NAACP Charges Wallace Job Bias," *Atlanta Journal,* December 8, 1973, p. 5-B; "Jackson to Fill More Jobs With Blacks, Women," *Atlanta Journal,* March 27, 1974, p. 7-K.

7. U. S. Commission on Civil Rights, *Federal Civil Rights Enforcement Effort* (Washington, D.C.: Government Printing Office, 1970), p. 307.

8. U. S. Commission on Civil Rights, *One Year Later* (Washington, D.C.: Government Printing Office, 1971), p. 29.

9. *Ibid.,* p. 20.

10. Equal Employment Opportunity Commission, *Sixth Annual Report* (Washington, D.C.: Government Printing Office, 1972), p. 12.

11. For more details on individual manpower programs see Charles S. Bullock, III, "Expanding Black Economic Rights" in *Alternatives to Racism and Racial Inequality,* ed. Harrell R. Rodgers, Jr. (San Francisco: W. H. Freeman, 1975).

12. For a concise discussion of these programs see Neil M. Singer, "Federal Aid to Minority Business: Survey and Critique," *Social Science Quarterly* 54 (September 1973), 292–305.

13. Peggy Simpson, "OMBE Puts Stress on Management," *Atlanta Journal,* March 27, 1974, p. 14-G.
14. Frank G. Davis, *The Economics of Black Community Development* (Chicago: Markham, 1972), pp. 94–96; Earl Ofari, *The Myth of Black Capitalism* (New York: Monthly Review Press, 1970).
15. Arthur I. Blaustein and Geoffrey Faux, *The Star-Spangled Hustle* (Garden City, N.Y.: Anchor Books, 1972), p. 248.
16. Bullock, "Expanding Black Economic Rights," Table 3.
17. Computed from data in Department of Labor, *Manpower Report of the President* (Washington, D.C.: Government Printing Office, 1974), p. 269.
18. Mike Causey, "Government Minority Jobs Rise," *Atlanta Journal,* March 6, 1974, p. 8-C.
19. Joan W. Moore, *Mexican Americans* (Englewood Cliffs, N.J.: Prentice-Hall, 1970), p. 62.
20. Frank G. Davis, *The Economics of Black Community Development* (Chicago: Markham, 1972), pp. 98–110.
21. 1974 *Manpower Report of the President,* p. 53 is the source of fiscal 1973 data; 1973 *Manpower Report of the President,* p. 56 is the source of fiscal 1972 data throughout this section.
22. 1973 *Manpower Report of the President,* p. 55.
23. Fiscal 1973 data indicate that the WIN program, which was strongly endorsed by the Nixon Administration, was only moderately successful. Of 353,900 participants, only 136,800 got jobs, and of these, only 65,200 were continuously employed for 90 days. 1974 *Manpower Report of the President,* p. 132.
24. Sar A. Levitan, Garth L. Mangum, and Ray Marshall, *Human Resources and Labor Markets* (New York: Harper and Row, 1972), p. 358.
25. Vivian W. Henderson, "Manpower Development and Equal Employment Opportunities," in *Manpower Policy: Perspectives and Prospects,* ed. Seymour L. Wolfbein (Philadelphia: Temple University Press, 1973), p. 93.
26. Levitan, Mangum, and Marshall, *Human Resources and Labor Markets,* p. 357.
27. Computed from data in 1974 *Manpower Report of the President,* pp. 53 and 367.
28. Leon H. Keyserling, *How Well Is the Employment Act of 1946 Achieving Its Goal?* (Washington, D.C.: Department of Labor, 1966), pp. 8–9.
29. Roberta V. McKay, "Employment and Unemployment Among Americans of Spanish Origin," *Monthly Labor Review* 97 (April 1974), p. 13; U.S. Department of Commerce, *American Indians: 1970 Census of Population* (Washington, D.C.: Government Printing Office, 1973), p. 27.
30. U. S. Bureau of the Census, Current Population Reports, Series P-23, No. 48, *The Social and Economic Status of the Black Population*

in the United States, 1973, (Washington, D.C.: Government Printing Office, 1974), p. 17.

31. Ben J. Wattenberg and Richard M. Scammon, "Black Progress and Liberal Rhetoric," *Commentary* 36 (April 1973), 35–44. Wattenberg and Scammon are among the leaders of those noting improvements in black incomes. They contend that "a *majority* of black Americans" are in the middle class (p. 36, italics in original). A number of black spokesmen disagree with Wattenberg and Scammon's optimism. See "The Black Middle-Class 'Majority': Is It Enough," reprinted in the *Congressional Record,* 93rd Congress, 1st Session, 119 (June 4, 1973), pp. E 3686–3687; "NAACP Rebukes Jewish Magazine," *Atlanta Journal-Constitution,* June 17, 1973, p. 12-B.

32. U.S. Bureau of the Census, Current Population Reports, Series P-23, No. 46, *The Social and Economic Status of the Black Population in the United States, 1972* (Washington, D.C.: Government Printing Office, 1973), p. 34.

33. U. S. Department of Health, Education, and Welfare, *Findings of the 1971 AFDC Study: Part I Demographic and Program Characteristics* (Washington, D.C.: Government Printing Office, 1971), p. 3.

34. Before 1974, states set benefits for all categoric programs.

35. Department of Health, Education, and Welfare, *Welfare Myths v. Facts* (Washington, D.C.: Government Printing Office, n.d.).

36. Mitchell Ginsberg, quoted in *Report of the National Advisory Commission on Civil Disorders* (New York: Bantam Books, 1968), p. 457.

37. Richard Zeckhauser and Peter Schuck argue that the needs of the poor differ according to their suitability for employment. They recommend fundamentally different income maintenance programs for those who cannot work and for those who can. See "An Alternative to the Nixon Maintenance Plan," *The Public Interest* 20 (Summer 1970), 120–130.

38. Michael Jay Jedel and Duane Kujawa, "Barriers to Minority Employment," *Atlanta Economic Review,* 23 (November–December 1973), 30.

39. "Settlement 'Breakthrough for Women,'" *Atlanta Journal-Constitution,* June 9, 1974, p. 21-A.

40. CSC rejected a number of plans as inadequate; "Revise EEO Plans, U.S. Agencies Told," *Atlanta Journal,* February 14, 1973, p. 2-C.

41. Sar A. Levitan and Garth L. Mangum, "An Old Budget for New Legislation: Impact 1974," reprinted in the *Congressional Record,* 93rd Congress, 2nd Session, 120 (March 18, 1974), p. E 1528.

42. Keynote address by Vernon E. Jordan, Jr., in *Congressional Record,* p. E 5284.

43. Andrew Young, "Blacks and the Nixon Administration: The Next Four Years," *Congressional Record,* 93rd Congress, 1st Session, 119 (March 26, 1973), p. E 1823.

44. 294 U.S. 587 (1935); 347 U.S. 475 (1954).

45. Research sponsored by National Science Foundation Grants GS-38157 and GS-38158 to Charles S. Bullock, III and Harrell R. Rodgers, Jr.

46. U.S. Department of Housing and Urban Affairs, *1971 HUD Statistical Yearbook* (Washington, D.C.: Government Printing Office, 1972), p. 89.

47. Harrell R. Rodgers, Jr., and Charles S. Bullock, III, *Law and Social Change* (New York: McGraw-Hill, 1972); Kenneth M. Dolbeare and Phillip E. Hammond, *The School Prayer Decision* (Chicago: University of Chicago Press, 1971); Neal A. Milner, *The Court and Local Law Enforcement* (Beverly Hills, Calif.: Sage, 1971).

48. Leon Friedman, *Southern Justice* (Cleveland: Meridian Books, 1967).

CHAPTER FIVE

Desegregation: Successes and Failures

It is too early to determine if current efforts at racial integration justify the hope that they can produce racial tolerance and eliminate discrimination. Yet the frequently vengeful, and sometimes plaintive, cries that desegregation has been a bust necessitate an evaluation. Thus, in this chapter two tasks are undertaken: (1) a review of the evidence on the conditions under which racial contact between adults leads to positive results; and (2) an investigation of the impact of interracial education on black and white students.

Most scholars who have studied the impact of racial mixing carefully point out that *mere contact* between the races is not necessarily beneficial. As Pettigrew cautions: "Increasing interaction, whether of groups or individuals, intensifies and magnifies processes already underway. Hence, mere interracial contact can lead either to greater prejudice and rejection or to greater respect and acceptance, depending upon the situation in which it occurs."[1] After a thorough survey of the literature, Allport specified that ideal conditions for positive interracial contacts include pursuit of common goals, cooperative dependence, equal status, and affirmative institutional support.[2] Other studies have stressed the importance of these and other positive conditions if interracial contacts are to yield beneficial results.[3]

RACIAL CONTACT BETWEEN ADULTS

If we distinguish between interracial contact that occurs under positive or negative conditions, the research literature brims with evidence that positive conditions lead to improved interracial tolerance. A dramatic example is provided by a study of the integration of military units under combat conditions where soldiers had to depend on one another for survival. The study revealed that integration under these circumstances led to more positive racial attitudes on the part of both whites and blacks.[4] A self-selection process where the more tolerant whites might have sought out black contacts was not possible, because the black soldiers had been randomly assigned to units. Studies of integrated housing where individuals were randomly assigned to apartments yielded similar results. Whites living closest to black families (for example, those who had black neighbors next door and those who lived in the areas of the project with the most blacks) became more tolerant toward blacks than the whites who were separated from blacks in the housing project.[5] For example, Wilner and his colleagues reported:

> Whether we consider the initially more favorable or initially less favorable respondents, those who live near Negroes in a project are more likely than those living farther away to report neighborly contact, to anticipate that white friends in the project will approve of such contact, to have high esteem for the Negroes in the project, to approve of the biracial aspect of the project, and to have a favorable attitude toward Negroes in general.[5]

Other studies indicate the value of white contact with blacks of equal or even superior status. One study found that white members of the Merchant Marine who had sailed with equal-status blacks were more tolerant toward blacks than those who had not been on interracial voyages. The impact was additive—the more interracial voyages a white took, the more tolerant he became.[7] Additionally, a study of white policemen in Philadelphia found that those who had worked with equal-status black policemen were more disposed toward desegregation of their department.[8] Another study found that whites who had known black professionals were significantly less prejudiced than those who had known only unskilled blacks.[9] Last, a field experiment that required whites to visit the homes of prominent blacks resulted in improved attitudes on the part of the white participants.[10]

Wilner and his colleagues, after surveying some thirty studies involving interracial contact, provided insight into the conditions under which racial mixing yields positive results.

> The cumulative evidence of these studies seems to provide rather substantial support for the general hypothesis that equal-status contact between members of initially antagonistic ethnic groups under circumstances not marked by competition for limited goals or by strong social disapproval of intergroup friendliness tends to result in favorable attitude change.[11]

Several studies, however, have found desegregation leading to negative or intensified racist attitudes when there is perceived competition between whites and blacks over scarce resources, such as housing or even political dominance. For example, whites living in neighborhoods that were experiencing a high influx of blacks were more negative toward blacks than whites who lived in all-white neighborhoods.[12] Obviously the whites felt pressured or threatened by the movement of blacks into their neighborhood. Rogin has argued that many white residents of Gary, Indiana, who had worked and lived around blacks for years, voted for George Wallace because they feared that the large and active black population in that city would control the political process.[13]

This short survey reveals that under some conditions interracial contact can lead to positive changes, but under other conditions contact produces negative results. Additional information on this topic is provided later in this chapter when we consider the impact of an integrated school environment on the attitudes of black adults.

SCHOOL INTEGRATION

School integration is often viewed as a device for improving the academic achievement of black students. The thrust of this view is that if school desegregation does not result in higher academic achievement for blacks, it is a failure and should be abandoned. This reasoning is faulty on several counts. First, the Supreme Court's decisions on school desegregation were based on the finding that black Americans were segregated because they were considered inferior by white society. To allow such discriminatory treatment, the Court said, denied black Americans the equal protection of the law. The obligation to desegregate the public schools, then, was based on a legal principle guaranteed to all Americans by the Constitution, not on a pedagogic speculation.

Second, it would be extremely peculiar if school desegregation had to prove its value as an academic device to justify its continuation. Segregated schools existed for decades without any demands that their existence be justified on any ground other than the pernicious doctrine of white supremacy. Third, to center attention almost exclusively on the academic potential of school desegregation neglects a number of other areas in which desegregation may have important consequences for society. The more important product of school desegregation may be improved race relations and life opportunities for black students. In this chapter we evaluate a number of potential benefits and costs of school desegregation.

The Academic Impact

Although academic improvement is not the best standard for evaluating desegregation, available evidence indicates that under proper conditions school integration does have some potential for enhancing the academic achievement of *both* white and black children. To evaluate the academic potential of school integration we must start with an examination of the factors empirically identified as predictors of school achievement. The most important factor found by the Coleman study was the child's home environment, defined as the education and socioeconomic status of the child's parents.[14]

Several characteristics of the school environment were also found to have some importance. High-quality classroom instruction, as measured by the presence of skilled teachers, was found to be weakly but positively related to student achievement. The socioeconomic status of the student body, however, was found to be the most important school factor affecting achievement. A middle-income environment seemed to be important because of the well-known *peer effect*. The values, aspiration levels, work habits, and achievement levels of the more socially prestigious members of a group tend to be emulated by the others.[15] As Pinderhughes has said:

> [W]hat the pupils are learning from one another is probably just as important as what they are learning from the teachers. This is what I refer to as the hidden curriculum. It involves such things as how to think about themselves, how to think about other people, and how to get along with them. It involves such things as values, codes, and styles of behavior.[16]

These findings are important because many black children can be placed in a middle-income milieu only in an integrated environment. Given the economic inequality between black and white Americans, most black children are in a lower-income milieu where the quality of instruction and the achievement level of their classmates may be very low. In lower-income schools, it is not uncommon for teachers to contribute to low achievement levels by averaging down their expectations,[17] producing a self-fulfilling prophecy.[18]

It is not surprising, therefore, that the Coleman study indicated that moving children to middle-income schools might have a considerable educational impact. For example, the study reported that black students who attend integrated schools score higher on achievement tests than segregated blacks, especially if they are in a middle-income environment with skilled teachers. Black students attending a school that is majority white are the highest achievers, especially if the white students are from middle income families.[19] A study that closely followed the Coleman Report found that "when disadvantaged Negro students are in class with similarly situated whites . . . , their average performance is improved by more than a full grade level. When they are in class with more advantaged white students . . . , their performance is improved by more than two grade levels.[11]

The importance of the income level of a student's peers is further attested to by the improved performance of disadvantaged blacks who attend schools with more advantaged blacks.[21] However, the gains made by integrating advantaged and disadvantaged blacks are less than the gains made when disadvantaged blacks are integrated with similarly situated whites. Consistent with this last finding, Wilson reported that even after controlling for family social class and school social class, blacks in majority white classrooms achieved significantly better than segregated blacks.[22]

Some have interpreted these findings to mean that the racial composition of the classroom has an independent impact on black achievement. The research is inadequate to prove this point, but it seems doubtful that black children learn better simply because they are in a classroom with white children. Traditionally a stigma has been associated with all-black schools, and considerable research indicates that segregation has a negative effect on the self-image of black students.[23] Thus, it is not surprising that Coleman found that blacks in desegregated schools tended to have a better sense of personal efficacy in the form of greater confidence in being able to master their environment, and that high personal efficacy was positively correlated with achievement. However, it is not clear that this phenomenon is now so important. Recent studies have tended to emphasize the importance of the improved curriculum and milieu of the integrated school.

The Coleman Report and many of the earlier studies have been disputed on a number of methodological grounds, one of which is that they were cross-sectional rather than longitudinal.[24] Coleman and many of the other authors lacked pretest data. Thus, it is impossible to know whether, because of a special selection bias, black students in desegregated schools were brighter than the blacks in segregated schools. Methodological problems notwithstanding, Wilson replicated the Coleman design using both cross-sectional and longitudinal data. Wilson found that, even controlling for differences among students entering a school, students (black and white) placed in schools with higher socioeconomic status peers showed the greatest achievement gains.[25] Recently Christopher Jencks reanalyzed the Coleman data on northern sixth grade students and concluded that the value of socioeconomic integration was even more substantial than originally believed.

> Poor black sixth graders in overwhelmingly middle-class schools were about 20 months ahead of poor black sixth graders in overwhelmingly lower-class schools. Poor students in schools of intermediate socioeconomic composition fell neatly in between. The differences for poor white sixth graders were similar.[26]

When Jencks controlled for the education of the children's families, he found that "poor white sixth graders in middle-class schools scored ten months ahead of poor white sixth graders in lower-class schools; and poor black students in middle-class schools continued to score almost twenty months ahead of similar children in disadvantaged schools."[27] Thus, Wilson and Jencks' analyses support Coleman's conclusion that the socioeconomic status of a classroom is the most important school factor affecting achievement.

In the Wilson study, however, there was no evidence that the racial mix of the classroom was important. Some might interpret this finding as an argument against integration. If the socioeconomic status and quality of instruction of a school are the most important school factors affecting achievement, these conditions might be met without desegregation. This argument overlooks the importance of positive interracial contacts for improved race relations. And it ignores the gross economic inequality between the races that makes it impossible for most blacks to be provided with a middle-income milieu in a segregated school.

Recent School Integration Studies

A review of the more recent studies of school integration programs provides somewhat better insight into the total impact of racial mixing in the schools. Before we begin this survey, however, it should be pointed out that several analyses of recent school integration studies have revealed that most of them suffer serious methodological problems,[28] and that the conditions for positive interracial change are rarely controlled for or investigated.[29] In other words, it is frequently difficult to know if positive or negative conditions for interracial contact are present in the schools being investigated. In addition, most studies have tried to assess the impact of integration after only one to three years, which is undoubtedly too short a time. Integration is frequently a traumatic experience and it probably takes several years for students to feel secure in, and fully adapt to, their changed environment. Only after five or six years of an integrated experience, therefore, can really solid studies be done. Despite these limitations, the studies generally reveal that black students in racially mixed schools make gains over those left in segregated schools.[30]

The best of these research projects administer standarized achievement tests to black students in segregated schools, and then retest the same students later, making a distinction between those who were bused to integrated schools and those left in segregated schools. Of such studies one review concluded: "The 'before and after' studies of the desegregation of school systems or individuals suggest that following desegregation, of whatever type or at whatever academic level, subjects generally perform no worse, and in most instances better."[31]

Even though some studies have found no improvement in the achievement of blacks and others have revealed only minor gains, no study of which we are aware has found that the achievement level of black children decreases with integration.[32] It is also extremely rare for studies to reveal any decrease in white achievement when schools are integrated. In those schools in which significant increases in black achievement were not found, we do not know if any of the conditions for positive change were present. Pettigrew and his colleagues have argued, however, that when at least some positive conditions are present, improvements are frequently found:

> The achievement of white and especially of black children in desegregated schools is generally higher when some of the following critical conditions are met: equal racial access to the school's resources; *classroom*—not just school—desegregation . . . ; the initiation of desegregation in the early grades; interracial staffs; substantial rather than token student desegregation. . . ; the maintenance of an increase in school services and remedial training; and the avoidance of strict ability grouping.[33]

Another review arrived at the same tentative conclusion:

> Though as yet unsupported by adequate field research, the most plausible hypothesis is that the relationship between integration and achievement is a conditional one: the academic performance of minority group children will be higher in integrated than in equivalent segregated schools, providing they are supported by staff and accepted by peers.[34]

Another survey of recent studies concludes that racial integration is generally beneficial to black students, but suggests that the most important factors besides a positive racial environment are classroom socioeconomic integration and early desegregation. Black children who begin their integrated school experiences at the elementary level experience the greatest gains in achievement. By the junior high or high school years it may be more difficult to overcome educational disadvantages.[35]

Interestingly, a few studies report that both black and white achievement levels increase significantly in racially mixed schools.[36] It may seem strange that the achievement of white students would improve when they are placed in a classroom with black students, many of whom may be low achievers. A logical explanation may be that a panic mentality set in motion by integration helps account for these improvements. A 1967 study found that, when integration takes place, school officials frequently try to compensate for the arrival of minority students by making special efforts to improve the curriculum and teaching for *all* students.[37] It is also possible that when schools are integrated, both black and white parents become concerned about their childrens' performance (for fear that they may fail or that they will not learn as much) and are more conscientious about seeing that children complete their homework. Pettigrew has additionally argued that integration allows cross-racial comparisons that may improve the self-image of both white and black students and thus lead to increased self-confidence and higher achievement.[38] This is an interesting argument but one supported by little research.

A few studies have found a slight decrease in the grade averages of integrated blacks, but the decrease is never very substantial.[39] At least one study found that the grades of black students increased with integration.[40] These findings probably mean simply that no significant changes take place because grading standards may differ substantially among schools. Some studies also show that the aspiration levels of blacks decrease slightly after integration, but this is not necessarily a negative finding.[41] Some black students have exaggerated and rigidly high aspiration levels. Research indicates that moderate aspiration levels are best for learning, and in some situations in which a decrease has been found, the new level may still be sufficiently high.[42] It is not uncommon to find that black aspirations went down after integration but achievement went up.[43] Still, there is little doubt that some black students find integration a disturbing, even defeating, experience. The important point, however, is that the academic impact of desegregation on both black and white students is usually positive.

Racial Tolerance

The impact of racial mixing in the public schools on racial tolerance is difficult to evaluate. Schools have often been desegregated under very tense and negative conditions, and this variable has rarely been examined in longitudinal studies. One study revealed that in hundreds of desegregated schools, the most invidious kinds of discrimination persist.[44] Given the number of racially mixed schools in which discrimination and tension remain, it is not surprising that some studies have found that desegregation has not led to increased interracial tolerance, or that in some cases desegregation has been viewed as disappointing by both black and white students.[45]

Still, the available cross-sectional evidence reveals that interracial contact frequently leads to racial tolerance, especially if conditions for positive change are present. For example, one study reported the rather obvious finding that blacks attending integrated schools where no racial tensions were present were more positive in their racial attitudes than black students in racially tense desegregated schools.[46] Several studies reveal that both black and white students who had attended interracial schools are more inclined than students without this experience to prefer to attend racially mixed schools in the future.[47] Further, students attending racially mixed schools are more inclined to say they trust and feel at ease around members of the opposite race.[48] Additionally, a study of 252 desegregating school districts during the 1970–

1971 school year found: "About 70 percent of the blacks and about 60 percent of whites agreed that both races were becoming more open-minded as a result of interracial busing."[49] A larger study of 879 schools in desegregating districts during the 1970–1971 school year also reported basically positive findings:

> Forty-one percent of students attending desegregated schools for the first time reported changes for the better on "going to school with students of another race," while only 5 percent reported changes for the worse. Eighty percent of students interviewed agreed that "students are cooperating more and more as the year goes on."
>
> While 33 percent of black students and 23 percent of white students said they would rather go to another school if they could, only 6 percent reported they did "not like it here" and 80 percent reported learning more in school than the previous year. A substantial majority of teachers and principals reported improvement in interracial relationships among students, and only 2 percent reported worsening relationships.[50]

In addition, black adults who attended interracial schools are more inclined to say that they would like their children to attend integrated schools and to prefer integrated neighborhoods.[51] Thus, in general, interracial contact can have positive implications for race relations, and this would undoubtedly be true more often if more consideration was given to providing a positive environment for integration efforts.

Life Opportunities

Perhaps the one finding that all studies (both longitudinal and cross-sectional) of interracial schools agree on is that the life opportunities of blacks improve considerably if they attend a racially mixed school. Blacks who attended interracial schools are more likely to graduate from high school, more likely to attend college and to attend a better college, and more likely to obtain a better job and receive a higher income.[52] Crain speculates that black gains in jobs and income probably do not result primarily from the educational gains made in racially mixed schools. Instead, he argues, blacks attending interracial schools learn to deal with and trust whites, which may improve their ability to succeed in their post-school environment. Crain also points out that, because many jobs are obtained through informal social contacts, blacks in an interracial environment have an advantage in obtaining a better job.

In summary, one fact seems clear: The record for integrated schools is generally positive, especially given the lack of attention to the creation of a favorable environment for interracial schools. Not only do blacks frequently achieve better in integrated schools, but blacks attending interracial schools are generally more trusting and tolerant of whites, and white attitudes are also more positive. The life opportunities for blacks are so improved that on this point alone integration would seem justified.

The Attack on School Integration: The Armor Study

Given these findings, it might be surprising that school integration has been under attack by some academicians. These attacks stem from unrealistic standards combined with flawed methodology. The chief antagonist of integrated education, David Armor, has argued that school integration has failed on a number of counts and thus should be terminated. Armor called only for termination of integration achieved through mandatory busing programs. But he has not actually studied induced busing programs, and so his thrust is actually directed at all school integration. Armor's attack hinges on a number of faulty premises, the first of which is that judges, legislators, and social scientists have maintained that "mere contact" between the races will lead to improved achievement, aspirations, self-esteem, and life opportunities for blacks while improving interracial tolerance.[53] This reasoning fails on two counts. In rendering school desegregation decisions, the Supreme Court relied, not on social science research that showed that "mere contact" between the races led to improvements, but on research that revealed that segregation had a very negative impact on black self-esteem, achievement, aspirations, and life opportunities. Armor makes no attempt to refute these findings.

Second, as pointed out earlier, social scientists have not argued that "mere contact" between the races will lead to positive change. They have argued that under the type of conditions specified by Allport integration can be beneficial. Armor relies on Allport's research, but distorts and reduces Allport's theory to a "mere contact" specification and then bases his research and expectations on this intellectual mutation. Thus, Armor does not test the assumptions of social science about the impact of integration at all. In defense Armor says: "My critics' argument that the programs I looked at did not fulfill the proper conditions for integration is beside the point."[54] But the argument is not beside the point. No one would have expected the programs to produce the changes Armor anticipated unless the conditions were fulfilled, and they were not. Also, Armor does not conclude from his studies that induced busing should be combined with the fullfillment of the proper conditions for positive change. He argues that all induced integration should be terminated, implying that induced integration *per se* is bad and unworkable. Nothing in his or anyone else's research warrants this conclusion.

Even if the prerequisites of Allport's contact theory had been present in the schools Armor studied, he could not have obtained evidence on the effects of integration because his methodology was inadequate. Given Armor's research design, the only way to determine if integration assists blacks is to compare (on a pretest–posttest basis) those who are bused with similar blacks who are left in segregated schools. If, using the proper controls, the integrated blacks show significant improvements over segregated blacks, the assumptions are verified. Even Armor seems to realize this, but lacking the proper data he compared the bused blacks with their white classmates.[55]

Comparing bused blacks to their white classmates will show a number of things, but it will not show whether blacks have benefited from integration. Yet, Armor argues that induced integration should be terminated because, during the short study period, the gains made by black students in integrated schools were not large enough to bring them up to the level of their white peers. This, of course, is not a valid standard for evaluating integration. As we have noted, studies of integration frequently reveal that integrated blacks have made achievement gains greater than those made by segregated blacks, and often the gains are quite significant. The gains achieved by blacks in integrated schools may not be enough to overcome in a few years all the educational differences between the races, but the additional gains normally found could be "the difference between functional illiteracy and marketable skills."[56] Surely this is a significant improvement. Pettigrew and his colleagues make this point forcefully:

> We believe it to be unrealistic to expect any type of educational innovation to close most of the racial differential in achievement while gross racial disparities, especially economic ones, remain in American society. Furthermore, we know of no social scientist who ever claimed school desegregation alone could close most of the differential. We are pleased to note the many instances where effective desegregation has apparently benefited the achievement of both black and white children, and where over a period of years it appears to close approximately a fourth of the differential.[57]

Armor further argues for terminating integration by busing, even though blacks may improve in integrated schools, because frequently a gap remains between their performance and that of their white peers. Armor argues that this gap might cause serious psychological harm to blacks and this might outweigh any beneficial effects of integration.[58] The gap in achievement levels should be of concern but probably not for reasons suggested by Armor. The only way the black students would feel vastly inferior to the white students would be if *all* the blacks did poorly and *all* the white students excelled. Obviously this would be unusual. Normally, in any class some blacks will do well and some whites will fail. Thus, the black students will have positive referents within their group. Armor's study provides a good example of this phenomenon. A sixth of the black junior high students in his study were such high achievers that they could not have shown improvement during the study period because they initially scored "virtually as high as the achievement test scoring allowed."[59]

Perhaps three conclusions can be drawn from this analysis. First, available evidence does not warrant final conclusions about the total potential of school integration. Little research has been done, much of the research suffers methodological problems (some manifest severe problems), and although the evidence basically favors integration, the research findings in some areas are frequently mixed. Thus, arguments that school integration should be terminated are premature and unjustified by available research. More important, these arguments are usually narrowly oriented toward the academic impact of integration. The focus needs to be broadened and lengthened to a consideration of the potential of integration for black–white relations in our society.

A second implication is that too little attention has been given to seeing that integration occurs in a positive environment. Courts and administrators should make every effort to see that desegregation plans embody as many of the conditions of Allport's contact theory as possible. Simply believing that contact alone will produce desirable ends will frequently produce inadequate, or even disappointing, results.

A third implication is that the gap between the achievement of blacks and whites in integrated schools should not be ignored. It is both encouraging and important that integration frequently improves black performance. The fact that improvements may be made indicates that specially trained teachers, working in creative integrated environments, can probably erase a substantial part of this gap. This should be especially true if integration begins at the earliest grades and if progress simultaneously continues in other areas of civil rights.

The Role of Quality Schools: The Jencks Study

A second attack on school integration has been based on biased interpretations of a study by Christopher Jencks and his colleagues, in which they explore factors explaining the economic differences between adults.[60] Some distorted the thesis of the book to conclude that school desegregation and quality schools are of no benefit. What Jencks and his colleagues really argued was that factors such as quality of education, cognitive skills, genes, home background, and IQ explain only about 25 percent of the variation between the income levels of individuals. They were unable to explain the other 75 percent of the differences, but they speculated that perhaps luck and personality were the important variables. Luck, they suspected, might be important in determining whether a person will be in the right place at the right time or will have beneficial contacts. Personality would determine how well an individual deals with colleagues, customers, and superiors. Because the authors felt that much of the difference in individual incomes was explained by factors that could not be influenced by schools, they argued that economic inequality should be dealt with by eliminating all forms of discrimination and by restructuring the American system to achieve a socialist society in which capital resources are more equally distributed.

The study did not attack quality schools or school desegregation. The authors said, in fact, that "the case for or against desegregation should not be argued in terms of academic achievement. If we want a segregated society, we should have segregated schools. If we wanted a desegregated society, we should have desegregated schools."[61]

Neither did the authors disparage efforts to equalize school resources. Jencks and his colleagues primarily wanted to make the point that school reform alone cannot equalize economic levels. However, the study does express reservations about the ability of school desegregation or remedial programs to greatly alter the achievement levels of students. If school resources were completely equalized, the authors believed that the test scores of deprived students would increase by only 9 to 19 percent. This, of course, would be no small accomplishment, but it would not equalize all groups. The authors also believed that current research warrants the conclusion that desegregating the schools would have a positive impact on black students' achievement levels, but that an educational gap would remain between the races. Moreover, it was suggested that achievement gains by blacks would improve only by 20 to 30 percent. However, for all the reasons discussed earlier, available research does not warrant writing integration off as having only minor potential at this time for achieving academic gains.

Also, the reservations expressed by Jencks and his colleagues about remedial programs seem premature, because all the study could show was that the teaching techniques and curricula *presently in use* do little to equalize educational performance. But too little attention has been paid to training teachers to deal with educationally handicapped children, and few school systems provide specific facilities or curricula to deal with serious learning problems. Common sense dictates that a concerted effort to deal with educationally handicapped children, along with faster progress in improving the social and economic conditions of black Americans, would produce significant progress. Even Jencks and his colleagues recognize this problem:

> In concluding this discussion we must again emphasize one major limitation of our findings. We have only examined the effects of resource differences among existing public schools. This tells us that if schools continue to use their resources as they now do, giving them more resources will not change

children's test scores. If schools used their resources differently, however, additional resources might conceivably have larger payoffs.[62]

The experience with Head Start programs indicates that even special programs will be of little value if students are given remedial help (frequently by untrained teachers) and then sent back into a depressed school environment.[63] Available evidence seems to indicate that special programs will be successful only in an environment in which high standards, highly trained teachers, and appropriate curricula are continually present. An innovative biracial program in St. Louis exemplifies how first-rate remedial programs can produce dramatic results.[64] In a special HEW program, highly qualified teachers work with classes of fifteen underachieving children. Achievement tests show that second and third graders make an average gain of a year and a half in one year, an 80 percent increase in rate of learning. Students in the fourth, fifth, and sixth grades average a fourteen-month gain in twelve months—a 50 percent increase in learning rate. Similar programs in Hartford and Cheshire, Connecticut, and in Berkeley, California, have achieved similar dramatic results.[65] For a number of reasons, therefore, Jencks and his colleagues may have seriously underestimated the value of special educational programs. Some remedial programs do succeed, and racial-socioeconomic integration may have a significantly higher potential than present studies indicate.

Even the argument by Jencks that schools cannot affect factors such as luck and personality is not very persuasive. For establishing important contacts, the advantages of attending a prestigious school are too obvious to belabor. Also, studies previously cited—of the life opportunities of blacks in interracial versus segregated schools—indicate that factors such as luck and personality may even be affected by the racial mix of a school. This is true because blacks in racially mixed schools may develop more contacts that lead to jobs, and they may learn to trust whites and to deal with them more easily than blacks who attend segregated schools and have less contact with whites.

In conclusion, then, Jencks and his colleagues did not argue that schools are unimportant or that good schools do not provide students with important advantages. As Mosteller and Moynihan observe, only the "simple of mind and heart"[66] could conclude from studies such as those reported by Jencks that schools do not make a difference. Jencks and his colleagues emphasized the need for the equalization of school resources and the value of good schools. A recent study by Guthrie and colleagues reviews eighteen separate studies that reveal that communities with more money have better schools, that students in high quality schools learn more, and that the graduates of advantaged schools obtain better jobs and earn higher incomes.[67] It is critically important, therefore, that *all* students receive the best educations possible. Because the financial structure of public schools is based primarily on the property tax and because blacks typically live in poor neighborhoods, it is obvious that the only way most black students will be provided with high quality schools is by integration. Thus, while Jencks' goal of a more equitable distribution of financial resources as a means of reducing inequality is admirable, we can hardly imagine its achievement in anything approaching the near future. While the theorists plot, therefore, the goal of integration must proceed.

SUMMARY

The ultimate goals of school integration are long range. Racial attitudes and behavior cannot be changed easily or over a short period of time. Therefore, until integration has been given a much longer and more carefully designed trial, no final conclusions can be reached about its total implications. However, the research surveyed here, although tentative, is basically positive. It seems clear that interracial education, especially when implemented under positive conditions, is beneficial. In many ways integration is a necessary preparation for interracial living. As a black parent in Rochester, N.Y., said about integrated schools: "Education . . . is preparing yourself to live and work in the world, and in this respect your education is definitely lacking if you are not being prepared to live and work with all types of people."[68] Jencks and his colleagues make a similar point:

> The most important effects of school desegregation may be on adults, not on students. School desegregation can be seen as part of an effort to make blacks and whites rethink their historic relationship to one another. If blacks and whites attend the same schools, then perhaps they will feel more of a stake in each other's well-being than they have in the past.[69]

A select committee of the United States Senate recently made the point even more forcefully.

> It is among our principal conclusions—as a result of more than two years of intensive study—that quality integrated education is one of the most promising educational policies that this nation and its school systems can pursue if we are to fulfill our commitment to equality of opportunity for our children. Indeed, it is essential, if we are to become a united society which is free of radical prejudice and discrimination.[70]

Besides the benefits of integration described in this chapter, in Chapter 6 we examine the changes that have taken place in white attitudes towards blacks since the 1940s. The evidence reveals a consistent, and sometimes dramatic, moderation. The alterations have primarily been caused by legally compelled desegregation. Despite the old saw that "you can't change men's hearts with law," experience indicates that laws that have required integration have led to changes in even deep-rooted attitudes. By requiring behavioral change, laws eventually serve as catalysts for new attitudes. Behaving differently, in other words, frequently leads to thinking differently.[71] In an excellent book, William Muir has reminded us that laws have always played an important role in shaping the attitudes of citizens. As Muir points out, law is a sensitive agent of social change. It educates, inculcates, and changes our attitudes.[72] Thus, the careful design and application of laws can aid considerably in achieving additional progress in race relations.

NOTES

1. Thomas F. Pettigrew, *Racially Separate or Together?* (New York: McGraw-Hill, 1971), p. 275.
2. Gordon W. Allport, *The Nature of Prejudice* (Cambridge, Mass.: Addison-Wesley, 1954), p. 267. A distinction between integration and desegregation is frequently made in the research literature. Desegregation is generally defined as simply racial mixing, and integration refers to positive interracial contact. We feel that some distinction needs to be made, but because we often cannot determine which situation exists, we use the terms interchangeably; and, where possible, we make a distinction between racial mixing that occurs under positive and under negative conditions.
3. See the studies reviewed in Daniel M. Wilner, Rosabelle Price Walkley, and Stuart W. Cook, *Human Relations in Interracial Housing: A Study of the Contact Hypothesis* (Minneapolis, Minn.: University of Minnesota Press, 1955), pp. 155–161.
4. S. A. Stouffer, et al., *Studies in Social Psychology in World War II*, vol. 1, *The American Soldier: Adjustment During Army Life* (Princeton, N.J.: Princeton University Press, 1949), chap. 10. A considerable literature on this topic is surveyed in Charles C. Moskos, Jr., "Racial Integration in the Armed Forces," *American Journal of Sociology* 72 (September 1966), 132–148.
5. See M. Jahoda and P. West, "Race Relations in Public Housing," *Journal of Social Issues* 7 (1951), 132–139; Morton Deutsch and Mary Evans Collins, *Interracial Housing: A Psychological Evaluation of a Social Experiment* (Minneapolis, Minn.: University of Minnesota Press, 1951); and E. Works, "The Prejudice-Interaction Hypothesis From the Point of the Negro Minority Group," *American Journal of Sociology* 67 (July 1961), 47–52.
6. Wilner, Walkley, and Cook, *Human Relations in Interracial Housing*, p. 95.
7. I. N. Brophy, "The Luxury of Anti-Negro Prejudice," *Public Opinion Quarterly* 9 (Winter 1945), 456–466.
8. W. M. Kephart, *Racial Factors and Urban Law Enforcement*

(Philadelphia: University of Pennsylvania Press, 1957), pp. 188-189.

9. B. MacKenzie, "The Importance of Contact in Determining Attitudes Toward Negroes," *Journal of Abnormal and Social Psychology* 43 (October 1948), 417-441.

10. F. T. Smith, "An Experiment in Modifying Attitudes Toward the Negro," *Teachers College Contributions to Education*, 1943, No. 887. Cited in Allport, *The Nature of Prejudice*, p. 267.

11. Wilner, et al., *Human Relations in Interracial Housing*, p. 4.

12. B. M. Kramer, "Residential Contact as a Determinant of Attitudes Toward Negroes" (Ph.D. dissertation, Harvard University, 1951); Lillian B. Rubin, *Bussing and Backlash* (Berkeley and Los Angeles: University of California Press, 1972), p. 65; Robert A. Dentler and Constance Elkins, "Intergroup Attitudes, Academic Performance, and Racial Composition," in *The Urban R's*, eds. Robert A. Dentler et al. (New York: Frederick A. Praeger, 1967), pp. 61-77; and Harvey L. Mohotch, *Managed Integration: Dilemmas of Doing Good in the City* (Berkeley and Los Angeles: University of California Press, 1972), pp. 174-204.

13. Michael P. Rogin, "Wallace and the Middle Class: The White Backlash in Wisconsin," *Public Opinion Quarterly* 30 (Spring 1966), 98-108.

14. James Coleman et al., *Equality of Educational Opportunity* (Washington, D.C.: Government Printing Office, 1966). The importance of these vectors differed according to the race of the student. The average of standardized regression coefficients for black students was: family, .25; facilities and curriculum, .11; teacher, .12; student body, .18. For the white students the coefficients were: family, .37; facilities and curriculum, .07; teacher, .08; student body, .09. See, James S. Coleman, "The Evaluation of Equality of Educational Opportunity," in *On Equality of Educational Opportunity*, eds. Frederick Mosteller and Daniel P. Moynihan (New York: Vintage Books, 1972), p. 161.

15. See, for example, O. J. Harvey and Jeane Rutherford, "Status in the Informal Group: Influence and Influencibility at Different Age Levels," *Child Development* 31 (June 1960), 377-385; and Kenneth P. Langton, "Peer Group and School and the Political Socialization Process," *American Political Science Review* 61 (September 1967), 751-758.

16. Cited in *Racial Isolation in the Public Schools*, a Report of the U.S. Commission on Civil Rights (Washington, D.C.: Government Printing Office, 1967), p. 82.

17. *Ibid.*, p. 105; See also R. Rosenthal and L. F. Jacobson, *Pygmalion in the Classroom: Self-Fulfilling Prophecies and Teacher Expectations* (New York: Holt, Rinehart, and Winston, 1968).

18. See Jonathan Kozol, *Death at an Early Age* (Boston: Houghton Mifflin, 1967).

19. U.S. Commission on Civil Rights, *Racial Isolation in the Public Schools*, p. 108.

20. *Ibid.*, p. 91.

21. *Ibid.*

22. *Ibid.*, pp. 98 and 99.

23. For a literature review see: Max Deutscher and Isidor Chein, "The Psychological Effects of Enforced Segregation: A Survey of Social Science Opinion," *The Journal of Psychology* 26 (May 1948), 259–287.

24. See, for example, R. C. Nichols, "Schools and the Disadvantaged," *Science* 154 (December 1966), 1312–1314; Samuel Bowles and Henry Levin, "The Determinants of Scholastic Achievement: An Appraisal of Some Recent Evidence," *Journal of Human Resources* 3 (Winter 1968), 1–24; and Henry S. Dyer, "School Factors and Equal Educational Opportunity," *Harvard Educational Review* 38 (1968), 38–56. Although the deficiencies of cross-sectional research are serious, we are even more concerned with the problem of multicollinearity which frequently exists in both the cross-sectional and longitudinal studies surveyed in this chapter. The multicollinearity problem results from the fact that the studies (including the Coleman Report) do not include adequate numbers of students who are from low SES families but attend first-rate schools, or students from high SES families who attend poor schools. Without this type of variance we are not convinced that the impact of high quality schools, innovative curriculums, or skilled teachers can be identified.

25. Research by Alan Wilson cited in U.S. Commission on Civil Rights, *Racial Isolation in the Public Schools,* pp. 165–256.

26. Christopher S. Jencks, "The Coleman Report and the Conventional Wisdom," in *On Equality of Educational Opportunity,* eds. Mosteller and Moynihan, p. 104.

27. *Ibid.*, pp. 86 and 87.

28. Nancy St. John, "Desegregation and Minority Group Performance," *Review of Educational Research* 40 (February 1970), 111–134; Robert P. O'Reilly, ed., *Racial and Social Class Isolation in the Schools* (New York: Frederick A. Praeger, 1970); Meyer Weinberg, *Desegregation Research: An Appraisal* (Bloomington: Phi Delta Kappa, 1968); and Gary Orfield, "School Integration and Its Academic Critics," *Civil Rights Digest* 5 (Summer 1973), 2–10.

29. Thomas F. Pettigrew, et al., "Bussing: A Review of the Evidence," *The Public Interest* 30 (Winter 1973), 91–93.

30. *Ibid.*, p. 93–98.

31. St. John, "Desegregation and Minority Group Performance," p. 127.

32. Pettigrew et al., "Bussing: A Review of the Evidence," p. 107.

33. *Ibid.*

34. St. John, "Desegregation and Minority Group Performance," p. 128.

35. *Toward Equal Educational Opportunity,* The Report of the Select Committee on Equal Educational Opportunity, United States Senate (Washington, D.C.: Government Printing Office, 1972), p. 217.

36. See the studies cited by Pettigrew et al., "Bussing: A Review of the Evidence," p. 98.
37. *Racial Isolation in the Public Schools*, p. 161.
38. Pettigrew, *Racially Separate or Together?*, p. 66.
39. Pettigrew et al., "Bussing: A Review of the Evidence," p. 107.
40. Edward B. Morrison and James A. Stivers, "A Summary of the Assessments of the District's Integration Programs, 1964–1971," Research Report No. 9 of Series, 1971–1972, Sacramento, California.
41. David Armor, "The Evidence on Bussing," *The Public Interest* 28 (Summer 1972), 101–102.
42. Pettigrew et al., "Bussing: A Review of the Evidence," pp. 107–108.
43. *Ibid.*
44. *The Status of School Desegregation in the South 1970,* A Report by the American Friends Service Committee; Delta Ministry of the National Council of Churches; Lawyers Committee for Civil Rights Under Law; Lawyers Constitutional Defense Committee; NAACP Legal Defense and Educational Fund, Inc.; and the Washington Research Project.
45. Charles S. Bullock, III and Mary Victoria Braxton, "The Coming of School Desegregation: A Before and After Study of Black and White Student Attitudes," *Social Science Quarterly* 54 (June 1973) 132–138; Mary Victoria Braxton and Charles S. Bullock, III, "Teacher Impartiality in Desegregation," *Integrated Education* 10 (July–August 1972), 42–46; Armor, "The Evidence on Bussing," pp. 102–105.
46. U. S. Commission on Civil Rights, *Racial Isolation in the Public Schools,* pp. 157–158.
47. *Ibid.,* p. 110.
48. *Ibid.,* p. 111.
49. Cited in Select Committee on Equal Educational Opportunity, *Toward Equal Educational Opportunity,* p. 210.
50. *Ibid.,* p. 229.
51. U. S. Commission on Civil Rights, *Racial Isolation in the Public Schools,* pp. 111–113.
52. Robert L. Crain, "School Integration and Occupational Achievement of Negroes," *American Journal of Sociology* 75 (January 1970), 593–606; Robert L. Crain, "School Integration and the Academic Achievement of Negroes," *Sociology of Education* 44 (Winter 1971), 1–26: Pettigrew et al., "Bussing: A Review of the Evidence," pp. 110–111.
53. Armor, "The Evidence on Bussing," pp. 92–93.
54. David J. Armor, "The Double Double Standard: A Reply," *The Public Interest* 30 (Winter 1973), 124.
55. Armor, "The Evidence on Bussing," p. 97.
56. Pettigrew et al., "Bussing: A Review of the Evidence," p. 96.
57. *Ibid.,* p. 99.

58. Armor, "The Double Standard: A Reply," p. 121.
59. Pettigrew et al., "Bussing: A Review of the Evidence," p. 103.
60. Christopher Jencks, et al., *Inequality: A Reassessment of the Effect of Family and Schooling in America* (New York: Basic Books, 1972).
61. *Ibid.*, p. 106.
62. *Ibid.*, p. 97.
63. See, for example, Office of Economic Opportunity, *Project Head Start: Evaluation and Research Summary 1965–1967* (Washington, D.C.: Government Printing Office, 1967).
64. Carter Smith, "Lagging Pupils Gain in City's Rooms of 15," *St. Louis Post Dispatch*, November 24, 1972, p. 11A.
65. Cited in Select Committee on Equal Educational Opportunity, *Toward Equal Educational Opportunity*, pp. 24 and 25.
66. Mosteller and Moynihan, eds., *On Equality of Educational Opportunity*, p. 21.
67. James Guthrie et al., *Schools and Inequality* (Boston: Massachusetts Institute of Technology Press, 1971).
68. U. S. Commission on Civil Rights, *Racial Isolation in the Public Schools*, p. 159.
69. Jencks et al., *Inequality: A Reassessment of the Effect of Family and Schooling in America*, p. 156.
70. Select Committee on Equal Educational Opportunity, *Toward Equal Educatioinal Opportunity*, p. 3.
71. See Pettigrew, *Racially Separate or Together?* pp. 278–280.
72. William K. Muir, Jr., *Prayer in the Public Schools: Law and Attitude Change* (Chicago: University of Chicago Press, 1967), pp. 122–138.

CHAPTER SIX

Political and Racial Attitudes: Black versus White

As we have noted, efforts to correct racial inequality in the past twenty years have produced some considerable progress, especially in voting and public accommodations. In education, employment, and particularly housing, progress has been more modest. Although many black Americans have gained substantially from civil rights efforts, the lives of millions of blacks—particularly those in urban ghettos and rural areas—have probably been affected very little by the limited sweep of this struggle. Additionally, the full promise of change that was widely perceived in the civil rights bills of the early and mid-1960s, and in the oration of Presidents Kennedy and Johnson and other national leaders, has not been realized by most black Americans.

In this chapter we assess some of the political and social implications of the perceived extent of progress in this area. First, we attempt to determine how the attitudes of black Americans have been affected by progress and failure in civil rights. For example, how do black Americans evaluate the amount of change in civil rights and what are the implications of their evaluations? Have black Americans become embittered toward the political system, political leaders, whites, integration, and peaceful political change, or does faith spring eternal? Second, we seek to determine if changes in civil rights have been accompanied by alterations—positive or negative—in white racial attitudes. Last, we discuss some of the implications of our findings. Specifically, we weigh the possibility of future racial conflict and reflect on the importance of the racial issue in future elections.

BLACK POLITICAL ATTITUDES: RIOTERS VERSUS NONRIOTERS

Perhaps nothing more dramatically expressed the mood of some blacks than the more than two hundred riots and hostile outbursts in American cities during the 1960s.[1] The important question is—how representative were the riots of feelings in the black community? Were the riots the work of a small number of blacks engaged primarily in criminal actions, or were they significant political events reflecting widespread frustration and anger in the black community? Furthermore, what does the recent relative calm indicate? Are black Americans becoming more satisfied with their position in society and the actions of the government, or do old resentments smolder and grow? The first question can be answered in two ways: (1) by determining the extent of participation in and support for the riots in the black community; and (2) by comparing the characteristics and attitudes of the rioters with those of the larger black community to determine if the rioters reflected the mood and characteristics of the black community or if they were basically social deviants.

The Riots

The evidence reveals that the riots were not simply manifestations of criminal behavior by a tiny fraction of the black community. Surveys indicate that between 11 and 20 percent of the ghetto residents in various communities participated in the riots.[2] Additionally, surveys generally reveal extensive support for the riots in the black community.[3] For example, in 1966 the Harris poll asked black Americans if they "thought the race revolt was supported by the rank and file of Negroes." Ninety-one percent answered affirmatively.[4] More specifically, a study of fifteen major cities in 1968 revealed that 54 percent of the blacks interviewed were in sympathy with the riots.[5] Similarly, Gary Marx reported than an average of 50 percent of the blacks surveyed in five cities believed that riots "do some good because they make whites pay attention to the problems of Negroes."[6] Another study showed that more than half of those blacks who said they would not join a riot sympathized with the aims and frustrations of those who would.[7]

Sympathy for the riots is also revealed by the evidence that blacks tended to blame them on specific grievances such as racial discrimination in housing, employment, and education. For example, a 1967 survey asked blacks what they considered the major reasons for riots. The primary reasons offered were: (1) lack of progress in giving blacks equality (72 percent); (2) lack of decent housing (67 percent); (3) lack of jobs (67 percent); (4) unequal educational systems (61 percent); and (5) police brutality (49 percent).[8] Additionally, blacks were asked if the stores that were looted during the riots had been charging Negroes exorbitant prices? Fifty percent of the respondents agreed, and only 14 percent disagreed.[9] Thus, as one study concluded: "most blacks, regardless of background characteristics, tend to perceive the riots as a form of protest rather than simply destruction or anomic behavior."[10] Blacks believed that future riots could be avoided only by ending racial discrimination and by improving the economic and political conditions of minorities.

When asked about the long-term consequences of the riots, blacks expressed mixed feelings. In some cities considerable proportions of the black population thought the riots might be harmful in the long run, but in others the majority sentiment was positive.[11] A 1967 nationwide survey revealed that 50 percent of the black population did not view riots as essentially harmful to the cause of civil rights.[12] Another nationwide survey of blacks in 1969 found that "two-thirds agree that at least some and perhaps most of the rioters have been good citizens. And, good guys or bad, justified or not, Negroes believe (by 40 to 29) that the riots have helped more than they have hurt —that, much as it saddens the majority to say so, rioting works."[13]

The Characteristics of Rioters

The riffraff theory of the riots is discredited by an examination of those who participated in the riots. Rather than being the hard-core unemployed or delinquents, the average rioter was a young male who was somewhat better off than his peers. Although there were only slight differences between rioters and nonrioters in employment, education, and income, the rioters were slightly better off. Nonetheless, rioters tended to be high school dropouts, were generally employed in jobs below their skill level, and had a history of moving in and out of the job market.[14] The rioters also tended to be more interested in their community and in civil rights activities than nonrioters.[15]

It is not surprising that the rioters were not the most deprived group in the ghetto, because numerous studies find that both support for riots and militancy increase with income and education. Caplan observed that "there is a significant relationship between schooling, militancy, and riot activity, but it is the militants and rioters who are better educated."[16] Campbell and Schuman also found that, of those blacks most inclined to say they would support a riot, 59 percent expressed satisfaction with their housing, 57 percent reported no personal experience with job discrimination, and 63 percent said they had white friends.[17] Marx found that militancy on the part of blacks was positively related to social status, education, social activity, social mobility, and cultural involvement.[18] On the other hand, the blacks least inclined to participate in protest activity were those who manifested low racial pride and little dissatisfaction, even though they were the most objectively deprived.[19] Thus, it is not surprising that the rioters were not a proletariat up in arms.[20] As Caplan has said:

> Apparently, continued injustice and the severe withdrawal of resources increase a deprived group's dependency behavior and approval of those who control scarce resources. These findings argue strongly against an "underclass" or strictly economic interpretation of militancy and violent protest in the ghetto.[21]

Although there are slight but important demographic differences between rioters and nonrioters, the factors that best distinguish the rioters are attitudinal and psychological. For example, numerous studies revealed that the rioters had much higher aspirations than nonrioters, and they tended to manifest much higher levels of personal efficacy. They were also inclined to believe that the American social and political system was keeping them from obtaining their goals.[22] Rather than blame their plight on personal inadequacies, they tended to believe that they had the ability to get ahead in the world were it not for discrimination. Crawford and Naditch specifically tested this blocked opportunity theory of riot behavior by combining measures of powerlessness with Rotter's internal-external scale. Caplan summarizes the results of this and other studies:

> They found that the most militant respondents were characterized by a high sense of personal efficacy and a low control over external forces that affect the probability of achieving personal goals. Employing a similar analytical framework, Garin et al. . . . found a marked tendency for militancy among Negro students to be associated with the belief that they could not reach personal goals because of external or social systemic constraints.[23]

Blacks who blamed their plight on personal inadequacies, such as a lack of job skills or a poor education, were most inclined to be politically passive.

Confidence In The Political System

Indications are that distrust of the political system and political figures is generally widespread in the black community. The rioters seemed to be only slightly more disaffected from the political system than the general black population. For example, when asked if the local government could be trusted to do what is right, 44 percent of the Newark rioters and 34 percent of the nonrioters said "almost never." In Detroit, 42 percent of the rioters and 20 percent of the nonrioters felt that anger with politicians was a major cause of the riot in that community.[24] Campbell and Schuman also reported that in fifteen cities "Negroes were consistently less satisfied with the efforts of all three governmental levels than whites, especially of their city mayor."[25] A 1968 study revealed severe alienation from the political system on the part of a large proportion of the black population: 61 percent felt that "what I personally think doesn't count very much"; 52 percent said that "people running the country don't really care what happens to people like me"; 52 percent felt that "almost nobody understands the problems facing me"; and 43 percent admitted that they "feel left out of things."[26]

The black population generally, and rioters especially, are alienated from the police. Generally the black population feels that the police provide their community with poor services while treating black people discourteously and even cruelly. In a national survey in 1969, 58 percent of the blacks under thirty felt that police brutality was a fact of life.[27] As noted in Chapter 2, the Kerner report revealed that incidents involving the police triggered many of the riots and that the black population manifested considerable animosity toward the police in all the cities studied. In Newark, for example, 71 percent of the rioters and 49 percent of the nonrioters felt that anger with the police had something to do with the riot.[28]

Another indication of black political alienation is the large number of blacks who say that this country is not worth defending. When asked if they thought "the country was worth fighting for in the event of a major world war," 39 percent of the Detroit rioters compared to 16 percent of the nonrioters answered negatively. In Newark, 53 percent of the rioters and 28 percent of the nonrioters thought the country was not worth the sacrifice.[29] A 1969 national survey reported that black Americans, by a margin of 56 to 31, felt that they should not fight the war in Vietnam because they are discriminated against in America.[30]

The culmulative evidence, then, indicates that while distrust, despair, and resentment toward the political system and its agents were more pronounced among rioters than nonrioters, they were pervasive in the black community.

Attitudes Toward Integration

Despite the anger and distrust of the black community, studies in the 1960s revealed that neither the majority of black Americans nor most rioters had racist or separatist ideologies. For example, Sears found little support for militant black leaders or separatism among rioters in Watts.[31] Similarly, Aberbach and Walker found that acceptance of the black power slogan did not imply a separatist orientation.[32] In Detroit, Aberbach and Walker reported an emerging racial ideology in the black community, but it was not separatist in nature. The ideology consisted primarily of a favorable interpretation of black power and a call for speedy and substantial efforts to improve the condition of all black people.[33]

Studies throughout the 1960s also revealed that the vast majority of black Americans preferred racial integration. In a nationwide poll in 1969, 78 percent of the black respondents said they preferred integrated schools, 81 percent preferred an integrated work environment, and 74 percent said they preferred integrated neighborhoods.[34] In another study, black parents rejected the option of their children having only black friends by a margin of 19 to 1.[35] A study in 1960 revealed that black support for integrated schools had risen to 84 percent, and for integrated neighborhoods to 97 percent.[36] Even the most militant segment of the black population, young northerners, had not abandoned the goal of integration. A 1969 study concluded that: "The cause for perhaps three-quarters of their generation is still the old set of goals: No more or less than an equal chance at decent jobs, housing and education—within an integrated America."[37]

Still, black Americans generally, and rioters particularly, believe strongly that Negroes should take pride in their race and an interest in their culture and history. The goal of integration, of course, does not conflict with racial pride. As Campbell and Schuman concluded, "A substantial number of Negroes want both integration and black identity."[38] The Kerner report revealed that the average rioter was proud of his race, and was more likely than nonrioters to view blacks more favorably than whites.[39] Another study found that three out of four blacks viewed the phrase "Black is Beautiful" as a simple statement of fact.[40] And support for the teaching of black culture in the public schools is increasing among black parents.[41]

The emphasis on black culture and identity have seemingly had a considerable impact on the black community. Until the 1960s, studies typically reported that black Americans tended to suffer from low self-esteem and a lack of racial pride. Well-known studies revealed that black children tended to choose a white over a black doll when asked to pick the "nice" or "pretty" doll.[42] The use of skin lighteners was also a sign of black self-hate. Increasingly studies find that these attitudes are disappearing. A recent replication of the doll studies revealed that 70 percent of the black children in a second and third grade sample choose the black puppet as the "nice puppet," 82 percent selected the black puppet as the one that is a "nice color," and 79 percent designated the white puppet as the one that "looks bad."[43]

Other studies reveal that blacks are now much less inclined to discriminate against one another on the basis of shades of blackness and that degree of skin color is no longer important in mate selection.[44] Increasingly blacks feel that they are a special people who share a spiritual quality, often designated as "soul", that sets them apart.[45] The increasingly positive self-image of black Americans contributes, of course, to their evaluation of their rightful place in American society and the obligations of the system to them.

Despite substantial support among black Americans for integration and the majority rejection of racism and separatism, a sizable minority has given up on white society. In a 1969 survey, 21 percent of the black respondents said they would prefer a separate black nation.[46] Hatred and distrust of the white man also seems to be substantially present in the black community. In Newark, 72 percent of the rioters and 50 percent of the nonrioters reported that at times they hated white people.[47] In the 1969 study cited above, 51 percent of the young blacks thought that white America wanted to keep them down, 69 percent of the black respondents felt that whites were either hostile or indifferent to their situation, and only 20 percent believed that whites really meant them well.[48] Campbell and Schuman found that a third of their black sample felt that whites were hostile and repressive and another third felt that whites were indifferent to their condition.[49]

Increasing numbers of blacks also express the feeling that they cannot achieve their rights without violence. Sears and Tomlinson reported that only 3 percent of the black residents of Watts thought violence would be necessary,[50] but Campbell and Schuman's study of fifteen cities disclosed that 15 percent of the black residents felt that violence would be required.[51] Two local studies in 1969 revealed that 31 percent and 41 percent of the black respondents believed that resort to violence would be necessary.[52] A national study in 1969 reported similar sentiments among 21 percent of the respondents, and another 25 percent of the respondents believed that Negroes should arm themselves. Among Northern blacks under thirty, "49 percent still believe that blacks can win their way peaceably, but an ominous 36 percent do not."[53]

This analysis provides a firm answer to our first question. The riots were definitely a form of political action that reflected considerable frustration with political, social, and economic conditions in America. The rioters were only slightly more racially conscious and disaffected from the political system than the black community. In addition to their age and sex (young males), rioters were best distinguished by a higher sense of personal efficacy and a belief that discrimination was holding them back and would continue to do so. Although the vast majority of black Americans maintained their faith in integration during the 1960s, impatience and distrust of white society was pervasive. The basic frustrations of the black community were reflected in the large number of blacks who believed that violence would be necessary to achieve future civil rights goals.

RECENT BLACK POLITICAL ATTITUDES

Our second question was whether black faith in the political system has grown or decreased during the relative calm following 1968. Considerable research indicates that the lack of recent riots does not reflect improved black confidence in the political system. Instead, black faith and confidence in the political system have declined seriously in the past few years. A 1969 study concluded that: "All the cheated hopes and false starts and bad advice have left black Americans a trace sadder, a bit wiser, several shades blacker—and more impatient now than they have ever been."[54] This same study showed that black confidence in the federal government's civil rights programs had dropped to 25 percent from a high of 74 percent in 1966. Another study showed that the percentage of blacks who said that progress in civil rights was going too slowly increased, from 43 percent in 1966 to 59 percent in 1969, and only 22 percent said they were satisfied with the pace of change.[55] The decline in black faith was also evidenced by a series of Harris polls that asked blacks if the federal government could be depended on to help blacks a great deal. During the Kennedy-Johnson era,

72 percent of the black respondents replied affirmatively; by 1971 positive responses have plummeted to 3 percent.[56]

Other indications of increasing black disaffection are numerous. Between 1966 and 1968, alienation scores for samples of blacks increased from 34 to 54 in comparison with an increase from 24 to 30 for the national sample.[57] During the same period, the proportion of blacks who doubted that they had as good a chance to succeed as others in society rose from 33 to 56 percent. In 1968, only 17 percent of the white sample held this negative outlook. Of a 1970 sample of black Vietnam veterans, 64 percent believed the real fight was in America, not Vietnam. Only 38 percent believed that weapons had no place in the domestic battle.[58]

The disaffection of the black population remains apparent into the early 1970s. Aberbach and Walker reported that "By 1971 distrust of the government was the norm for Detroit's black population."[59] A survey conducted by the University of Michigan found that 78 percent of black Americans believed that the government was run for the benefit of all in 1958; by 1970 the comparable figure was 34 percent.[60] Black disaffection was also expressed in a 1971 Gallup poll that pointed up a wide gap between the satisfaction levels of blacks and whites on a number of points. The figures below provide some examples:[61]

	Satisfied	
	White (percent)	Black (percent)
How satisfied are you with life in your community?	78	51
How satisfied are you with your job?	84	63
How satisfied are you with your income?	65	41
How satisfied are you with your housing?	77	51

Between 1970 and 1971, blacks became increasingly critical in their evaluation of whites. For example, in a longitudinal study of Detroit, Aberbach and Walker reported that "blacks' optimism about prospects of achieving a desirable pattern of race relations in the near future, which was widespread in 1967, had declined markedly by 1971.[62] In 1971, a majority of a national sample of blacks agreed with nine of ten negative statements about whites, with 81 percent stating that most whites consider blacks inferior. The number of blacks agreeing with the statement "Whites are really sorry slavery for blacks was abolished" rose from 63 to 70 percent between 1970 and 1971. By 1971, 68 percent of the black respondents said that whites have a mean and selfish streak, and 79 perecnt said that whites will give blacks a break only when forced.[63]

By 1972, a Harris poll found that 81 percent of the black population negatively evaluated the civil rights and race record of the Nixon administration. During the Johnson administration, 75 percent of the black population had expressed positive views toward government activities in civil rights. The number of blacks who said they looked to the national government for leadership in the civil rights area had shrunk from 67 percent in 1966 to 4 percent in 1972. Additionally, only 16 percent of the black population expressed "a great deal of confidence" in the executive branch, compared with 19 percent for Congress and 23 percent for the Supreme Court.[64]

As this is being written, black faith and confidence in the American political system, its leaders, and whites in general is very low. Blacks seem to feel left out of the political process and to feel that white America has turned its back on their problems. Still, surprisingly perhaps, black support for integration remains high. In 1972, 78 percent of a national sample of blacks said they would like to see the nation's schools desegregated.[65] A survey of 54,000 college-bound black students revealed that two-thirds believed that integration was necessary, but two-thirds also said that political authorities were unaware of the needs of black Americans and some 25 percent said that the condition of black Americans was worsening.[66]

Disaffection with the political system is also reflected in the attitudes of black school children. Studies of children's developing political attitudes have normally found that young white children manifest very positive attitudes toward the American political system and political authorities.[67] It is generally assumed that these early positive attitudes play an important role in determining how the mature adult will relate to the political system. In contrast with whites, black students are less positive toward the political system and political authorities; they are less politically efficacious and more politically cynical. Evidence indicates that the best predictor of blacks' efficacy and cynicism is their evaluation of their position in the political hierarchy. In other words, their political feelings do not reflect a sense of personal inadequacy, but rather seem to reflect black students' assessment of the realities of the political process.[68]

A number of studies have revealed that black school children are significantly more alienated toward the police than their white cohorts.[69] During the Kennedy-Johnson years black children seem to have had generally positive attitudes toward the national executive, but they did not feel that he was very helpful or powerful.[70] In the course of their education, black students become less attached to the American political community. These findings led Greenberg to hypothesize that as black adolescents "acquire increased political information, sophistication, and consciousness, they will demonstrate an increasing tendency to reject the national political community."[71]

Although evidence on the political attitudes of black school children is not all negative, it is clear that blacks leave the public schools more politically cynical, less politically efficacious, and less attached to, and supportive of, the political system and authorities than their white peers. As Clarke has observed, these attitudes should make young blacks ripe for apathy or unconventional political behavior, depending on the stimuli in their environment.[72]

THE RACIAL ATTITUDES OF WHITES

Although black attitudes toward whites are becoming increasingly antagonistic, white attitudes toward blacks seem to have improved considerably over the past thirty years. Surveys report a significant shift during this period in the attitudes of whites toward blacks and toward the goals embodied in the civil rights movement. For example, the number of whites who said they supported integrated transportation increased from 44 percent in 1942 to 80 percent in 1970. In the South, the increase during the same period was from 4 percent to 67 percent. By 1970, 75 percent of the general population favored school integration. Although only 48 percent of southern whites supported school integration, this was a considerable increase from 2 percent in 1942.[73] A Gallup poll in 1969 revealed that 78 percent of southern parents said they would not object to their children attending a school with a "few Negroes." In 1963, only 38 percent of southern parents had given this response. In 1963, only 17 percent of southern parents said they would not object to their children attending a school that was half black. By 1969 approval was registered by 47 percent of southern parents.[74]

A number of studies have revealed some moderation in traditional white stereotypes of blacks. The Harris survey in the next column shows some of these changes.

> ... the average white American in 1963 could live with integrated education and integrated parks, restaurants and hotels; he could accept, although just barely, a black dinner guest. In 1970 he was no longer concerned about having a black dinner guest and was no longer ready to totally reject the possibility of integrated neighborhoods.[76]

ERRATUM SHEET

Racial Equality in America: In Search of an Unfulfilled Goal
Charles S. Bullock III and Harrell R. Rodgers, Jr.

Pages 154 and 155:

The extract paragraph at the bottom of page 154 should follow the second line from the top of page 155.

The table at the top of page 155 should appear at the bottom of page 154.

Goodyear Publishing Company, Inc.
Pacific Palisades, California.

(C) 1975 by Goodyear Publishing Company, Inc.

On the basis of a number of surveys conducted from 1942 to 1970, the National Opinion Research Center concluded that:

	Agree 1963 (percent)	1971 (percent)
Blacks have less ambition	66	52
Blacks laugh a lot	68	48
Blacks smell different	60	48
Blacks have lower morals than whites	55	40
Blacks want to live off the handout	41	39
Blacks have less native intelligence	39	37
Blacks keep untidy homes	46	35
Blacks breed crime	35	27
Blacks care less for the family than whites	31	26
Blacks are inferior to white people	31	22

Although progress in the South was considerable, acceptance of integration was not as general as in the rest of the nation. The National Opinion Research Center surmised that in 1970 white southerners could accept integrated transportation, parks, restaurants, and hotels, and they leaned toward acceptance of integrated schools, but they rejected the idea of a black dinner guest or an integrated neighborhood.[77]

In a study of fifteen Northern cities in 1968, Campbell also found that considerable numbers of white Americans expressed positive attitudes toward blacks and integration. For example:

> 86% say they would not mind at all having a qualified Negro as a supervisor on the job,
>
> 69% think Negroes are justified in using orderly marches to protest against racial discrimination,
>
> 68% say they believe many or some Negroes miss out on good housing because white owners won't rent or sell to them,
>
> 67% say they favor laws to prevent discrimination against Negroes in job hiring and promotion, and
>
> 49% say they would not mind at all if a Negro family with the same income and education moved next door.[78]

The fact that large numbers of whites increasingly express positive attitudes toward blacks and integration cannot conceal the fact that white attitudes toward blacks are still frequently very negative. For example, despite the positive attitudes reported by Campbell, some negative attitudes were also uncovered. For example:

> 67% say Negroes are pushing too fast for what they want,
>
> 56% believe that Negro disadvantages in jobs, education, and housing are due mainly to Negroes themselves rather than to discrimination,
>
> 51% oppose laws to prevent racial discrimination in housing,
>
> 33% say that if they had small children they would rather they have only white friends, and
>
> 24% of those old enough to vote say they would not vote for a qualified Negro of their own party preference who was running for mayor.[79]

White attitudes toward urban riots and their causes were equally unsympathetic. Of Campbell's white respondents, only 11 percent said that the riots were not at least partially planned in advance. Fifty-two percent said the riots were mainly or partially a way of looting. When asked what should be done to prevent future urban disturbances, 47 percent favored stronger police controls.[80] In addition, a 1967 Harris survey (next column) found a wide gap between the perceptions of whites and blacks as to the reasons for the riots:[81]

Other studies have cast doubt on the commitment of white Americans to integration. In a nationwide study in 1970, white respondents were asked if they favored desegregation, strict segregation, or something in between. Seventeen percent of the sample chose strict segregation, 44 percent picked something in between, and only 35 percent opted for desegregation. In the same study, 78 percent of the black respondents said they favored desegregation.[82] A series of Gallup polls reveal similar negative findings. A 1968 nationwide Gallup poll asked whites:

"How well are blacks being treated?" Seventy-three percent said the same as whites. When asked if President Johnson was pushing integration too fast, 48 percent answered affirmatively. Fifty-eight percent also thought that blacks were primarily to blame for their condition.[83] In 1970 the Gallup poll asked whites if racial integration should be speeded up. Sixty-two percent said "no."[84]

	White (percent)	Black (percent)	Difference (percent)
Lack of good education for Negroes	46	61	+15
Lack of decent housing for Negroes	39	68	+29
Lack of jobs for young Negroes	34	67	+33
Lack of firmness by local mayors and governors	37	13	−24
Lack of progress in giving Negroes equality	30	72	+42
Hatred of whites by Negroes	33	20	−13
Desire of Negroes to loot stores	26	9	−17
Desire of Negroes for violence	23	13	− 9
Police brutality against Negroes	8	49	+41

White Americans tend to reveal a mixture of sympathetic and unsympathetic attitudes toward black Americans. As Campbell has said: "When interviewed they (white Americans) reveal a compromise of beliefs and opinions, some of them leaning toward the segregationist, unsympathetic, censorious side of the balance, others toward the integrationist, supportive, understanding side."[85] The average white, in other words, is both an integrationist and a segregationist. A sizable proportion of the white population will accept integration, but only up to a point. The social distance implied in the relationship is of considerable importance, with white attitudes toward integrated housing and intermarriage remaining the most resistant to change.[86] Furthermore, although many whites support integration in some context, they are reluctant to support the policies or tactics necessary to expedite progress.

The belief of a majority of white Americans that blacks are responsible for their conditions also indicates how invisible discrimination can be. Most white Americans accept no responsibility for the conditions of minorities, and efforts to compensate black Americans for three hundred years of slavery would be genuinely unpopular in the white community. Aberbach and Walker found, in fact, that many white residents of Detroit were openly hostile about what they perceived as special treatment for blacks by the government.[87]

We must conclude with Campbell that "the white population of this country is far from a general acceptance of the principle and practice of racial equality."[88] Pettigrew has estimated that about one-fifth of the white population has a strong personality commitment to racism.[89] This estimate is probably not exaggerated. From a look at the Harris poll showing the changes in white stereotypes of blacks (Table 6-2), it is clear that—even though positive changes have occurred—a majority of whites still believe that blacks ask for more than they are ready for and that blacks have less ambition than whites. Nearly half (48 percent) say that blacks laugh a lot and that blacks smell different. Thirty-nine percent believe that blacks want to live off the handout, 37 percent believe blacks have less intelligence, and 22 percent believe blacks are inferior to whites. The other surveys reported above indicate that on questions concerning almost any topic concerning integration, a core of whites opposes almost any efforts to achieve racial equality.

Pettigrew speculates that perhaps as many as three-fifths of the white population are conforming bigots—that is, they go along with policies that discriminate against blacks without being overtly prejudiced.[90] The lack of insight exhibited by large numbers of whites about the factors that discriminate against blacks, and about the general lack of support for vigorous attacks on discrimination, indicates that Pettigrew's point is well taken. On issues such as busing of school children to achieve desegregation, the conforming bigots may join the hard-core racists to form a solid majority.

In recent years considerable attention has been focused on what some have called a white backlash.[91] The backlash theory seeks to explain the lack of white support for vigorous civil rights measures, George Wallace's showings in northern industrial communities during the presidential primaries of 1968 and 1972, and Richard Nixon's appeal to the working class as a result of retreat to racism by once mildly sympathetic whites. The evidence provides little support for the theory. While the backlash was supposedly occurring (1966 to 1970), polls showed that white attitudes toward blacks were steadily improving. Pettigrew makes a well-reasoned argument that Wallace's showings in the North resulted from a high turnout of whites who were never sympathetic to blacks and from whites who voted for Wallace as a protest candidate, not because of his racist views. Pettigrew presents data to show that during the 1972 presidential primaries many northern white Republicans voted for Wallace because it was clear that Nixon would receive the nomination without their support, and because Wallace was a safe protest candidate because it was clear that he could not actually win.[92]

During the 1972 presidential election, however, the racial issue was extremely important, and there were signs that the white population was backing off slightly from its support for school integration. The public fear of busing to achieve racial desegregation was so exaggerated that it was politically risky for a candidate to support such measures. This was true even though only 3 percent of all busing is done for purposes of desegregation.[93] Nixon, however, fanned public fears by making an issue of busing and by arguing that children should attend their neighborhood schools. The Nixon campaign on busing may have had some short-term impact on white attitudes. For example, a 1971 national poll revealed that 75 percent of white Americans supported integrated schools. In November of 1972, however, one poll showed that only 46 percent of a national sample of whites supported school integration (compared to 78 percent of blacks). Whites opposed the busing of school children to achieve desegregation by a percentage margin of 81 to 14.[94] Similarly, in 1971 a Harris poll reported that 47 percent of the white population was willing to allow their children to be bused to an integrated school if such busing was ordered by a court. By 1972 only 25 percent were willing. A national poll late in 1972, however, revealed that 65 percent of whites and 80 percent of blacks supported school desegregation, but 73 percent of the whites opposed busing to achieve desegregation.[95] The lack of consistency in these polls probably resulted from differences in wording; some were clearly worded to distinguish between school integration and integration achieved by busing, but others were not. Some opponents of integration may not feel that it is socially acceptable to voice this attitude. However, opposition to busing may be a smoke screen for this sentiment. Also, some part of the population (approximately 10 percent) may have permanently reversed their attitudes on school integration.

Comparable data on other areas of integration are not available, and thus it is difficult to determine if any reversals have occurred in the public's attitude on other racial issues. Both Presidents Nixon and Ford have opposed busing to achieve school desegregation and it would not be surprising if some small attitudinal reversals have occurred in other areas as well. In tracing the recent history of white racial attitudes, Sheatsley has shown that white attitudes normally moderated only after a form of racial discrimination has been fought and overcome.[96] Thus, both crisis and the implementation of new policies are necessary to combat racist views. During the Kennedy and Johnson administrations the cloak of legitimacy was stripped from many racist policies, many programs were implemented, and surveys revealed that the public's attitudes improved considerably. During the Nixon administration, however, discrimination was not under vigorous attack, and the momentum of the civil rights movement was slowed. President Ford seems intent on continuing these policies. The result may very well be a slight reversal on the part of some whites whose attitudes had earlier begun to moderate. In addition, as black demands increase in the North, there may be additional decreases in white support.

SUMMARY AND IMPLICATIONS

This review indicates that the attitudes of both black and white Americans have changed considerably during the past fifteen years. The displaced dreams of black Americans, and the unfulfilled promises made to them have caused increasing impatience with the pace of civil rights, considerable bitterness toward white society, and presumably an historic low in black faith and confidence in the American political system and its leaders. It is not clear how much change has actually taken place in the racial attitudes of whites, nor is it clear whether whites will assume the role of amity, resistance, or rebuff in the future. But, generally, it seems that positive changes have occurred. Still, there remains an ominous breach between black and white Americans. While developing more negative attitudes toward whites, and less patience with and trust in the political system, blacks have also shed their debilitating self-stereotypes and now demand changes consistent with their new image. As Caplan has said:

> In the midst of squalor and despair, Negroes have abandoned the traditional stereotypes that made nonachievement and passive adaptation seem so natural. Rather, they have developed a sense of black consciousness and a desire for a way of life with which they can feel the same pride and sense of potency they now derive from being black.[97]

White America, however, seems ready to accept only a very slow rate of racial change. Those who hold such attitudes are blind to the most important transformation in the black community: the alteration in the self-image of black Americans. Black Americans no longer have the psychological mechanisms that allowed them to adapt to discrimination, subordination, and poverty in the past. Blocked opportunities, discrimination, and failure cannot be squared with the new black psyche, and black reactions to these phenomena can be counted on to differ substantially from past reactions.

An obvious question raised by these findings is whether the clash between black and white attitudes is likely to be manifested in more riots. The question cannot be answered definitively. Most theorists of revolt behavior predicted that while Richard Nixon was in office there would be no more riots.[98] The theory of relative deprivation predicts that violence occurs when there is a wide gap between the expectations of a group and their objective conditions. A group that is kept in a condition of continued suppression does not normally revolt. Revolt occurs when promises of relief and change are made, raising expectations and then not fulfilling them. These theorists argue that Nixon did not promise to improve the conditions of black Americans and that—expecting only neglect from him —they were willing to wait him out.

However, another theory predicts that violence erupts when the political trust of a group is low, and when that group believes that the use of violence in the past produced favorable goals.[99] As our survey has shown, the political trust of black Americans is very low, a sizable proportion of the black community believed that the riots were useful, and black feelings that violence may be necessary to achieve civil rights goals seem to be increasing. Thus, this theory would predict a considerable potential for future violence.

We do not find either theory persuasive. One must wonder if the hopes fueled in the 1960s could be so quickly extinguished by the election of Nixon. The second theory, with its heavy emphasis on political trust, would have predicted extensive unrest during recent years. We suspect that the right spark could set off more riots, but doubt that it will. Blacks seem to be interested at this time in working through the system. However, continued rebuffs could reverse this attitude.

Another implication of the data analyzed here is that

racial issues are likely to be of continuing importance in future elections. For a number of reasons, race is a dysfunctional electoral issue for those who support racial equality. In the past race as an electoral issue has been a catalyst for polarization and varying degrees of demagoguery. Analyses of Wallace voters reveal that they were characterized by three psychollogical variables: (1) prejudice toward blacks; (2) high feelings of fear and distrust; and (3) feelings of relative deprivation.[100] The average Wallace voter, who had little education but medium income, feared that his position in society was deteriorating and that blacks, because of special treatment, were making significant advances. As Pettigrew has said about Wallace supporters: "They have typically done better than their fathers and are objectively fairly secure: but, like black Americans, they have high aspirations without a sense of making progress toward their goals."[101] These feelings may be unfounded, but they reveal why campaign issues dealing with black needs tend to anger, frustrate, and frighten many whites.

To avoid polarization it is best that campaigns be directed toward programs for improving the lot of all Americans who suffer such conditions as poverty, joblessness, and poor educations. This approach makes sense because millions of whites suffer many of the deprivations that afflict millions of minority group members in America.

The other reason that race makes a divisive electoral issue is that some candidates can always be counted on to unscrupulously capitalize on white fears, prejudices, and hostilities. In 1968, Wallace's racist appeals netted him ten million popular and forty-five electoral votes. Undoubtedly he would have done better if Nixon had not encroached on the racist position with his southern strategy. Republican campaigners swept the South, promising that if Nixon was elected he would deemphasize civil rights—a sinister promise that was not neglected after his election. The result of the Nixon-Wallace effort was that 97 percent of all black voters, but only 35 percent of white voters, cast their ballot for Hubert

Humphrey. Converse and his colleagues concluded that the "presidential vote must have been as sharply polarized along racial lines as at any time during American history."[102]

In the 1972 election the polarization and demagoguery continued, and busing was a key issue. Wallace sought once again to exploit the racial issue and was attracting a considerable following before he was shot by a would-be assassin. Nixon substantially oriented his election toward public fears over busing, fears that he played a part in creating. The result was another racial split with 79 percent of the black voters but only 33 percent of the whites voting for George McGovern.

The cumulative evidence thus indicates that the continuation of race as an electoral issue is not a good sign. The result will probably be more polarization and political demagoguery, and the serious problems that plague all of society will be sacrificed to more emotional issues.

NOTES

1. See Bryan T. Downes, "Social and Political Characteristics of Riot Cities: A Comparative Study," *Social Science Quarterly* 49 (December 1968), 509.

2. David O. Sears and John B. McConahay, "Racial Socialization, Comparison Levels, and the Watts Riot," *Journal of Social Issues* 26 (Winter 1970), 121–140; Nathan Caplan and Jeffrey M. Paige, "A Study of Ghetto Rioters," *Scientific American* 219 (December 1968), 15–21. In this study only males between the ages of fifteen and thirty-five were interviewed in Newark, and 45 percent said they had participated in the riot.

3. Two excellent surveys of these studies are Nathan Caplan, "The New Ghetto Man: A Review of Recent Empirical Studies," *Journal of Social Issues* 26 (Winter 1970), 59–73; and James W. Clarke, "Race and Political Behavior," in *Comparative Studies of Blacks and Whites in the United States,* eds. Kent S. Miller and Ralph Mason Dreger (New York: Seminar Press, forthcoming 1974).

4. Data collected by Louis Harris and reported in Hazel Erskine, "The Polls: Demonstrations And Race Riots," *Public Opinion Quarterly* 31 (Winter 1967), 671.

5. Angus Campbell and Howard Schuman, *Racial Attitudes in Fifteen American Cities: Supplemental Studies for the National Advisory Commission on Civil Disorders* (Washington, D.C.: Government Printing Office: 1968), p. 47.

6. Gary T. Marx, *Protest and Prejudice* (New York: Harper and Row, 1969), p. 32.
7. Campbell and Schuman, *Racial Attitudes in Fifteen American Cities*, p. 10.
8. *Ibid.*, p. 66.
9. *Ibid.*, p. 65. See also Joe R. Feagin and Paul B. Sheatsley, "Ghetto Residents Appraisals of a Riot," *Public Opinion Quarterly* 32 (Fall 1968), 352–362; and Harlan Hahn and Joe R. Feagin, "Rank-and-File Versus Congressional Perceptions of Ghetto Riots," *Social Science Quarterly* 52 (September 1970), 363–365.
10. Clarke, "Race and Political Behavior," p. 29.
11. Thomas Crawford and Murray Naditch, "Relative Deprivation, Powerlessness, and Militancy: The Psychology of Social Protest," *Psychiatry* 33 (May 1970), 208–223; "Report From Black America," *Newsweek*, June 30, 1969, p. 22. See also David Sears and T. M. Tomlinson, "Riot Ideology in Los Angeles: A Study of Negro Attitudes," *Social Science Quarterly* 49 (December 1968), 490.
12. Robert Beardwood, "The New Negro Mood," *Fortune Magazine* 77 (1968), 146–152.
13. "Report From Black America," *Newsweek*, June 30, 1969, 23.
14. Caplan, "The New Ghetto Man," pp. 63–64.
15. Otto Kerner et al., *Report of the National Advisory Commission on Civil Disorders* (New York: Bantam Books, 1968), p. 113.
16. Caplan, "The New Ghetto Man," p. 63.
17. Campbell and Schuman, *Racial Attitudes in Fifteen American Cities*, p. 58.
18. Marx, *Protest and Prejudice*, p. 33.
19. Caplan, "The New Ghetto Man," 62.
20. "Report From Black America," p. 23.
21. Caplan, "The New Ghetto Man," 62.
22. See Crawford and Naditch, "Relative Deprivation, Powerlessness, and Militancy;" and Caplan and Paige, "A Study of Ghetto Rioters."
23. Caplan, "The New Ghetto Man," 70.
24. *Report of the National Advisory Commission on Civil Disorders*, p. 135.
25. Campbell and Schuman, *Racial Attitudes in Fifteen American Cities*, p. 41.
26. Data collected by Louis Harris and reported in Hazel Erskine, "The Polls: Negro Philosophies of Life," *Public Opinion Quarterly* 33 (Spring 1969), 152.
27. "Report From Black America," p. 21.
28. Kerner et al., *Report of the National Advisory Commission on Civil Disorders*, pp. 116–121 and 135.
29. *Ibid.*, p. 135.
30. "Report From Black America," p. 20.
31. David O. Sears, "Black Attitudes Toward the Political System

in the Aftermath of the Watts Insurrection," *Midwest Journal of Political Science* 13 (November 1969), 515–544.

32. Joel D. Aberbach and Jack L. Walker, "The Meaning of Black Power: A Comparison of White and Black Interpretations of a Political Slogan," *American Political Science Review* 44 (June 1970), 367–388.

33. Joel D. Aberbach and Jack L. Walker, "Political Trust and Racial Ideology," *American Political Science Review* 64 (December 1970), 1199–1219.

34. "Report From Black America," p. 19.

35. Campbell and Schuman, *Racial Attitudes in Fifteen American Cities*, p. 16.

36. Angus Campbell, *White Attitudes Toward Black People* (Ann Arbor, Mich.: Institute for Social Research, 1971), pp. 130 and 133.

37. "Report From Black America," p. 21.

38. Campbell and Schuman, *Racial Attitudes in Fifteen American Cities*, p. 6.

39. Kerner et al., *Report of the National Advisory Commission on Civil Disorders*, p. 133.

40. "Report From Black America," p. 22.

41. Campbell and Schuman, *Racial Attitudes in Fifteen American Cities*, p. 19.

42. See, for example, K. Clark and M. Clark, "Racial Identification and Preference in Negro Children," in *Readings in Social Psychology*, eds. T. Newcomb and E. Hartley (New York: Holt, 1947).

43. Susan Harris Ward and John Braun, "Self-Esteem and Racial Preference in Black Children," *American Journal of Orthopsychiatry* 42 (July 1972), 644–647. See also, Harrell R. Rodgers, Jr., "Racial Pride and Black Children: The Importance of Integrated Schools," *Integrated Education* (July-October 1973), 62-63.

44. J. Richard Utry, Karl E. Bauman, Charles Chase, "Skin Color, Status, and Mate Selection," *American Journal of Sociology* 76 (January 1971), 722–733.

45. "Report From Black America," p. 22.

46. *Ibid.*, p. 20.

47. Kerner et al., *Report of the National Advisory Commission on Civil Disorders*, p. 133.

48. "Report From Black America," p. 21.

49. Campbell and Schuman, *Racial Attitudes in Fifteen American Cities*, p. 6.

50. Sears and Tomlinson, "Riot Ideology in Los Angeles," p. 501.

51. Campbell and Schuman, *Racial Attitudes in Fifteen American Cities*, p. 9.

52. Both of the unpublished studies are cited in T. M. Tomlinson, "Determinants of Black Politics: Riots and the Growth of Militancy," *Psychiatry* 33 (May 1970), 248.

53. "Report From Black America," p. 19.

54. *Ibid.*

55. *Ibid.*
56. Clayton Fritchey, "Court Must Be Beyond Reproach," *Washington Post,* October 9, 1971, p. A–15.
57. Erskine, "The Polls: Negro Philosophies of Life," p. 152.
58. The study by Wallace Terry is cited in Gary Ronberg, "Black Veteran's Fight Isn't Over," *St. Louis Post-Dispatch,* March 15, 1973, p. 6A.
59. Joel D. Aberbach and Jack L. Walker, *Race in the City* (Boston: Little, Brown, 1973), p. 210.
60. Reported in *The New York Times,* November 5, 1971, p. 48.
61. *The New York Times,* September 26, 1971, p. 61.
62. Aberbach and Walker, *Race in the City,* p. 48.
63. Louis Harris, "Black Animosities Found Increasing," *Washington Post,* October 6, 1971, p. A-8.
64. Louis Harris, "Blacks, Whites Split on Issues Facing U. S.," *Atlanta Journal-Constitution,* November 23, 1972, p. 22-A.
65. *Ibid.*
66. *The New York Times,* April 4, 1972, p. 58.
67. The literature is considerable on this point. See, for example, David Easton and Jack Dennis, *Children in the Political System: Origins of Political Legitimacy* (New York: McGraw-Hill, 1969).
68. Harrell R. Rodgers, Jr., "Toward Explanation of the Political Efficacy and Political Cynicism of Black Adolescents: An Exploratory Study," *American Journal of Political Science,* 18 (May 1974), 257–282.
69. See, for example, Harrell R. Rodgers, Jr. and George Taylor, "The Policeman As An Agent of Regime Legitimation," *Midwest Journal of Political Science* 15 (February 1971), 72–86.
70. Edward S. Greenberg, "Children and Government: A Comparison Across Racial Lines," *Midwest Journal of Political Science* 14 (May 1970), 249–275.
71. Edward S. Greenberg, "Children and the Political Community: A Comparison Across Racial Lines," *Canadian Journal of Political Science* 2 (December 1969), 487.
72. Clarke, "Race and Political Behavior," p. 29.
73. Andrew M. Greeley and Paul B. Sheatsley, "Attitudes Toward Racial Integration," *Scientific American* 225 (December 1971), 13–19.
74. Cited in Pettigrew, *Racially Separate or Together?,* pp. 176–177.
75. Harris, "Black Animosities Found Increasing," p. A-8.
76. Greeley and Sheatsley, "Attitudes Toward Racial Integration," p. 15.
77. *Ibid.*
78. Campbell, *White Attitudes Toward Black People,* p. 4.
79. *Ibid.,* pp. 4–5.
80. *Ibid.,* pp. 17 and 29.
81. Erskine, "The Polls: Demonstrations and Race Riots," p. 666.
82. Campbell, *White Attitudes Toward Black People,* p. 136.
83. Data collected by George Gallup and reported in Hazel Erskine,

"The Polls: Opinion on Racial Problems," *Public Opinion Quarterly* 32 (Winter 1968), 699, 700, 702.

84. *The New York Times,* November 1970, p. 61.
85. Campbell, *White Attitudes Toward Black People,* p. 5.
86. Pettigrew, *Racially Separate or Together?,* p. 267.
87. Aberbach and Walker, "Political Trust and Racial Ideology," p. 1204.
88. Campbell, *White Attitudes Toward Black People,* p. 63.
89. Pettigrew, *Racially Separate or Together?,* p. 205.
90. *Ibid.*
91. Pettigrew, *Racially Separate or Together?,* pp. 165–203; Campbell, *White Attitudes Toward Black People,* p. 132; and Greeley and Sheatsley, "Attitudes Toward Racial Integration," p. 19. All reject the notion that a backlash has occurred.
92. Pettigrew, *Racially Separate or Together?,* p. 173.
93. *Fact Book on Pupil Transportation* (New York: Metropolitan Applied Research Center, 1972).
94. Harris, "Blacks, Whites Split on Issues Facing U. S.," p. 22-A.
95. Cited in *Toward Equal Educational Opportunity,* The Report of the Select Committee on Equal Educational Opportunity, United States Senate (Washington, D.C.: Government Printing Office, 1972), p. 207.
96. Paul Sheatsley, "White Attitudes Toward the Negro," *Daedalus* 95 (Winter 1966), 217–238.
97. Caplan, "The New Ghetto Man," p. 71.
98. See the discussion in Pettigrew, *Racially Separate or Together?,* pp. 147–157.
99. Edward N. Muller, "A Test of a Partial Theory of Potential for Political Violence," *American Political Science Review* 66 (September 1972), 928–959.
100. Pettigrew, *Racially Separate or Together?,* p. 241.
101. *Ibid.,* p. 250.
102. Philip Converse et al., "Continuity and Change in American Politics: Parties and Issues in the 1968 Election," *American Political Science Review* 63 (December 1969), 1085.

CHAPTER SEVEN

Racial Equality: Past, Present, and Future

The thought of an Indian raid in the third quarter of the twentieth century has an air of comic opera about it. Yet, in March of 1973 some two hundred militant Indians seized the town of Wounded Knee, South Dakota. By this deed the Indians hoped to dramatize their poverty and subjugation. For more than two months the Indians held the town and exchanged gunfire with federal marshals through the long nights. At about the same time Chicanos were organizing another lettuce boycott to bring attention to the slave labor conditions in which many field laborers work; and in St. Louis a black civil rights activist was urging ghetto thieves to shift their activities to the white suburbs. Percy Green, leader of this campaign, explained that only when enough whites suffered crime would something be done about the unemployment and poverty that drive blacks to lawlessness. During that same year George Wallace crowned a black Homecoming Queen at the University of Alabama, and Los Angeles, with a white majority, elected a black mayor.

These activities signify successes and failures in the continuing struggle to achieve racial equality in America. As this country prepares to celebrate its two hundredth birthday, the goal of racial equality is far from being achieved. Racist attitudes still prevail among white Americans, and minorities are still disproportionately poor and suppressed. Perhaps most serious is the unwillingness of most whites to accept responsibility for the conditions of minority Americans.

Despite these continuing problems, some very substantial progress has been made in the past twenty years. Achievements in voting, public accommodations, and school desegregation in the South have been considerable, even though not complete. In employment and welfare some conditions have been improved, but recently the rate of change has slowed and some reversals have occurred. Desegregation in housing does not meet even the tacky standards of tokenism. Still, if we learn anything from the recent past, it is that change can be achieved when sustained efforts are made.

It is difficult to say what the future essence and impact of civil rights efforts will be. Long before racism has been completely banished, the civil rights movement seems to have lost its luster, drive, and sense of urgency. As Julian Bond has said: "Black people have stopped being chic."[1] The lull seems to be the result of several things. Jim Crow laws which served as rallying standards for battle are gone. The racism that continues is generally institutional and too veiled to draw the determined outrage stimulated by cruder forms of discrimination. In addition, inflation, the Vietnam war, and the Nixon administration have diverted funds and white support from the movement.

Perhaps also the movement suffers from battle fatigue and seeks psychic retreat. Many of the important civil rights leaders of the 1960s are gone, and signs of division are evident among those who remain. "The new leadership of the 1970s is diffuse —a mosaic of moderators and militants, separatists and assimilationists, a handful of national celebrities and a thousand anonymous storefront organizations."[2] Many of the more important civil rights groups have also dissipated. The Student Nonviolent Coordinating Committee (SNCC) is completely gone, the Southern Christian Leadership Council has withered under the direction of Ralph Abernathy, and CORE is licking its wounds after trying to work with the Nixon administration.

The current strategies of the movement are as diverse as its leadership. The NAACP continues to employ litigation and lobbying; the Urban League interacts with the white power structure to obtain grants and programs; Jesse Jackson's movement (PUSH) in Chicago lobbies corporations for good jobs for blacks and more contracts for black businesses; Imama Amiri Baroka (formerly Le Roi Jones) preaches nationalism in New Jersey; and Bobby Seale is trying to work through the political process in Oakland. The movement, thus, has become more localized and is engaged in struggles with significant and highly intractable forms of discrimination. Economic progress is now the central concern of the movement, but this goal is stymied by the inflation and high unemployment that are rocking America in the early 1970s.

Many black leaders now believe that future progress depends on winning control of political positions and mobilizing votes at the polls. Recently black voters have elected many moderate to liberal whites as well as ever swelling ranks of blacks. As reported in Table 7-1, the partial data for 1964 show only 103 elected black officials in the nation. In 1974 there were 2,991—1,307 of whom were in the South.[3] Although no southern blacks have won statewide office, in 1974, 2 served in Congress, 60 served in state legislatures, and 46 were mayors. Hundreds served on the governing boards of counties, cities, and school districts.

Impressive as these gains are, blacks still experience substantial electoral setbacks at the state and local level. Lowndes County, Alabama, where Stokely Carmichael sought to organize the 80 percent black population in 1966, remains white dominated as black candidates won only one of eight races in 1972.[4] In Mississippi in 1971, black candidates sought a variety of offices, including the governorship. Of 309 black office-seekers, only 50 were successful, and none won the more significant local offices such as sheriff or chancery clerk.[5] Blacks control only 5 school boards and 3 county commissions, although they comprise a majority of the voting-age public in 56 southern counties. The failure of black candidates to win elections in areas in which they constitute a majority can be laid to fear, low black turnout, black votes being bought or not counted, massive white bloc voting when there is a serious black challenge, and alterations of election districts to dilute black strength.[6]

TABLE 7-1

Black Legislators and Blacks Elected to Other Public Office

	1964	1968	1970	1972	1974
TOTAL	103	1,125	1,860	2,264	2,991
United States Senate:					
United States	—	1	1	1	1
South	—	—	—	—	—
House of Representatives:					
United States	5	9	13	13	17
South	—	—	—	—	2
State Legislatures:					
United States	94	172	198	206	236
South	16	29	32	47	60
Mayors:					
United States	(NA)	29	81	86	108
South	(NA)	18	25	31	46
Other:					
United States	(NA)	914	1,567	1,958	2,629
South	(NA)	437	508	698	1,199

Sources: *The Social and Economic Status of the Black Population in the United States, 1972,* U. S. Department of Commerce (Washington, D.C.: Government Printing Office, 1973), p. 100. Various volumes of the *National Roster of Black Elected Officials* (Washington, D.C.: Joint Center for Political Studies).

To the extent that black votes have elected blacks and sympathetic whites, gains have been realized. At the very least the presence of significant numbers of blacks in the electorate reduces the most blatant forms of racism.[7] During the 1970s several southern governors have called for an end to racial discrimination—a far cry from the "never" response characteristic of the immediate post-*Brown* era.[8] Black congressman Andrew Young (D-Georgia) has perhaps best described the changes occurring in the treatment accorded black constituents by white politicians:

> When we had only 5 percent of the black vote registered, some white politicians would talk about the niggers. Then we registered 15 percent and the politicians would say nigra. When we had 40 percent registered, the word was Negro, and when the total reached 50 percent, the politicians were talking about "our black brothers."[9]

Also, as a result of new power at the polls, black communities are getting a larger share of public goods, especially of items requiring referenda. Black votes have been translated into paved streets, running water and sanitary sewers, garbage pick-up, fire stations, and a share of the nonmenial public and private jobs.[10]

Where black officeholders have been elected, the gains for the black community might be even greater. Certainly greater pride and a heightened sense of efficacy may be derived from the election of black officials. In predominantly white bodies—for example, state legislatures, city councils, or county commissions in majority white cities and counties—a single black or even a few blacks may be unable to engineer major changes, but they can raise issues of concern to their race that might not be voiced in their absence. In addition, a black Georgia legislator noted: "We also serve as watchdogs. We keep them honest and, by our mere presence, many (harmful) things that normally would be done are not."[11]

Two emerging conditions may eventually result in black representatives on predominantly white governing bodies having greater influence. First, as black officials gain seniority and interact with white colleagues, they may acquire both the acumen and the political debts that will enable them to wield greater influence.[12] Second, as Republican strength grows in the South, black legislators and councilmen may come to hold the balance of power in some bodies. Should this happen, black politicians may be in a position to extract significant policy concessions.

There are, however, severe hazards in depending too heavily on the minority vote for political change. There are only twelve major cities and twenty congressional districts in the nation in which blacks constitute 40 percent or more of the population. Mississippi is the only state in which blacks comprise more than 30 percent of the population.

In addition, even in those cities and counties in which blacks constitute a majority of the elected officials, they may be hamstrung by lack of financial resources and lack of control. Southern counties with black voting majorities tend to be particularly poor.[13] Major cities which blacks now, or will soon, dominate are also caught in the vice of declining tax bases and rising costs. In the face of rising financial needs, local governments are narrowly constrained in their ability to respond. State laws typically limit the taxing and borrowing authority of municipalities. Traditionally the federal government has helped overcome the needs of urban areas through categoric grants. The New Federalism of the Nixon administration altered this relationship by making block grants available for broad areas (for example, community development) rather than specific projects (such as urban renewal). Although the latitude offered users may be valuable, a drawback of general revenue sharing enacted in 1972 is that—because need is no longer a criterion—many large cities receive less money than they did through categoric aid. A second problem is that where revenue sharing funds are apportioned by local white officeholders, programs that benefit minorities may be less likely to be funded.

Financial limitations may not be the only obstacles confronting cities with black mayors. In many cities elected officials must share policy-making powers with bureaucrats. Matters such as municipal employment practices and educational policy may be partially shaped by unions. Professionals may give first allegiance to their colleagues rather than to elected officials. Other policies affecting a city may be made by a special district (for example, sewers) or by a metropolitan agency in which a black governed city may have little influence.

Another possibility is that black elected officials may be co-opted by the political system. Rather than support policies that would produce major changes, newly elected blacks may support more traditional policies designed to win acceptance from white power-holders. On the basis of a limited data base, Salamon found that many of the blacks recently elected in Mississippi are committed to accommodationist strategies that are unlikely to produce substantial policy changes.[14] Moreover, as blacks holding public office acquire a middle-class life style, they may also adopt middle-class values and gradually forget their less fortunate brothers.

If black elected officials are unable to produce improvements for their constituents, the consequences may be greater distrust of the political system and declining political support among blacks. As Leroy Johnson, black Georgia state senator, has said: "It's more difficult to be a black legislator than it is to be a white one. The reason is that black people expect more from their politicians than whites. They expect us to move the world."[15]

At the national level the limitations on the ballot as a method of achieving racial equality are terribly apparent. Obviously blacks constitute too small a portion of the electorate to win major national offices, but they may be an influential minority in close campaigns. The traditional identification of blacks with the Democratic party, however, allowed Nixon to use the race issue to scare the hard hat and southern white vote into his corner in the 1968 and 1972 elections. The result was that Nixon felt that he won office independent of black support and that he owed them little. And little is precisely what he delivered. Even at the height of the civil rights movement, blacks had little influence over the major federal policies that affected them (for example, housing and education policy[16]), but under Nixon they had even less influence. It is little wonder that black America, along with increasing portions of white America, felt alienated from the Nixon administration. Recently Vernon Jordan, director of the Urban League, was asked: What ever happened to black America? His answer reflected a pessimism nurtured by the day-to-day experience of trying to influence national policy: "It is still there, still struggling, still largely separate and unequal—and increasingly isolated from the centers of politics and power in America."[17]

We are, then, at an awkward stage in the civil rights movement. Some very important progress has been made, and at the local level additional gains are slowly being pieced together. At the national level blacks have little influence over decision making, and resentment is high. It is not clear whether progress will be made soon enough to ameliorate the increasingly hostile mood of minority Americans. In Chapter 6 we documented the unprecedentedly low political trust of black Americans, and their high level of hostility towards whites. Recent actions of American Indians and Chicanos indicate that they increasingly share the disaffected attitudes of blacks. Accompanying these attitudes have been significant increases in minority pride and self-confidence. In the long run this may prove to be the most significant change that occurred among minorities in the twentieth century. Once minorities have pride and self-confidence, they are unlikely to settle for anything but equality, regardless of the mood and commitment of white America.

The cost of continued racial inequality in American society is, of course, substantial. One price of continued resistance to minority equality could be more violence and strife. But regardless of whether more American cities are burned and more lives lost, the tensions and costs resulting from failure to eliminate racial inequality will be substantial. The principles on which American society is based will continue to be goals and promises, not deeds, and millions of Americans will live in anguish, poverty, and despair because they were denied opportunities for a decent life. And all of society will be poorer for it. American cities will continue to deteriorate because of a disappearing tax base as middle-class citizens (including middle-class minorities) flee to the suburbs to escape unresolved problems. Crime will continue to plague society as long as people are unemployed, ill housed, ill fed, ill educated.[18] And as long as racism and discrimination exist, hypocrisy will be the anathema of democracy.

No member of society, then, can escape the consequences of racism and repression. We live in a finite world in which the actions and conditions of all citizens are interrelated. Racism, poverty, and misery are man-made phenomena and they can be remedied by man; but they are not white problems or black problems, they are everyone's problems. As Whitney Young used to say: "We may have come here on different ships, but we're in the same boat now."

NOTES

1. The next several paragraphs draw heavily upon Peter Goldman, "Black America Now," *Newsweek*, February 19, 1973, p. 29.
2. *Ibid.*, p. 33.
3. Some point to the fact that blacks hold only about one-half of 1 percent of the elected offices in the country. This standard is misleading since blacks tend to be concentrated in core cities, North and South, and the rural South. A more meaningful standard might compare the number of black officeholders with the number of public servants elected by majority black constituencies.
4. "Alabama," *Atlanta Journal-Constitution*, November 19, 1972, p. 2-C.
5. Lester M. Salamon, "Mississippi Postmortem: The 1971 Elections," *New South* 27 (Winter 1972), 43–47.
6. *Ibid.;* Frederick M. Wirt, *Politics of Southern Equality* (Chicago: Aldine, 1970), pp. 169–171; *The Shameful Blight* (Washington, D.C.: Washington Research Project, 1972), pp. 93–135.
7. William Keech, *The Impact of Negro Voting* (Chicago: Rand McNally, 1968).
8. Bill Montgomery, "Governors Hinting New Day For The South,

Negro Days," *Atlanta Journal-Constitution,* February 7, 1971, p. 14-A. "Text of Carter Inaugural Talk," *Atlanta Journal,* January 12, 1971, p. 5-A.

    9. Lawrence Taylor, "Black Movement Alters Emphasis," *St. Louis Post-Dispatch,* April 1, 1973, pp. 1, 10-B.

    10. Keech, *Impact of Negro Voting.* But for an outstanding essay on the difficulties blacks, even when well organized, may encounter in obtaining relatively minor substantive goods, see, Michael Parenti, "Power and Pluralism: A View From the Bottom," *Journal of Politics* 32 (August 1970), 501–530.

    11. Robert De Leon, "Negro Elected Officials on Hot Seat," *Atlanta Journal-Constitution,* November 30, 1969, pp. 1, 18-C.

    12. For examples, see Jeff Nesmith, "Johnson Gains Proficiency, Efficiency," *Atlanta Journal-Constitution,* March 11, 1973, p. 12-C.

    13. Charles S. Bullock, III, "Southern Elected Black Officials" (Paper delivered at the Southern Political Science Association, Atlanta, Ga., November 1–3, 1973); Hanes Walton, Jr., *Black Politics* (Philadelphia: Lippincott, 1972), p. 200.

    14. Lester M. Salamon, "Leadership and Modernization: The Emerging Black Political Elite in the American South," *Journal of Politics* 35 (August 1973), 615–646.

    15. Nesmith, "Johnson Gains Proficiency, Efficiency," p. 12-C.

    16. Harold L. Wolman and Norman C. Thomas, "Black Interests, Black Groups, and Black Influence in the Federal Policy Process: The Cases of Housing and Education," *Journal of Politics* 32 (November 1970), 875–897.

    17. Goldman, "Black America Now," p. 31.

    18. See Ramsey Clark, *Crime In America* (New York: Simon and Schuster, 1970).